Baron Byng to Bagels:
Tales of Jewish Montreal

By Joe King

Author of
From the Ghetto to the Main:
The Story of the Jews of Montreal
and
The Jewish Contribution to the Modern World

Copy Editor: Heather Solomon-Bowden

Published by
The Montreal Jewish Publication Society
March, 2006

Cover, design and page layout by infoPlume
Printing by Imprimerie Larivière inc.

Other recent books by the author

From the Ghetto to the Main:
The Story of the Jews of Montreal

The Jewish Contribution to the
Modern World

Printed in Canada

Preface

Authors write the preface to their books—and virtually no one reads them (except that special breed of person called the proof-reader)—so I expect that, in writing this one, I am virtually talking to myself.

Why did I research and write this book? Well, first of all, this is really three books rolled into one.

Part One is a chronological history of Jewish Montreal, illustrated with what I feel are some exceptional prints, drawings and photographs.

Two good examples—the flyer printed by the Congregation Shearith Israel in New York congratulating the British on their capture of Canada, in 1760 (even the archivists hadn't heard of it) and the 1897 advertisement by the elegant Ogilvy's in Yiddish! Oy vey!

I feel that illustrations make a book of this nature come alive.

Part Two of this book is a blending of two elements—profiles of individuals and organizations, and some of the tales of Jewish Montreal I have collected through the years.

These are funny stories (to me, at least—and to the many audiences who come to hear me talk) and I am always in the market for more.

And once again, there is a stress on illustrations. I showed Hillel Becker—an authority on world champion figure skater Louis Rubenstein—a picture of Louis posing, in St. Petersburg, Russia, wearing the ribbon signifying he is the world's first champion fancy skater. This was a picture Hillel had never seen, so I feel, in some ways, I have widened the door to the past.

So, why did I write the book? It's because the response by Montrealers—tens of thousands of whom have scattered to the four corners of the world—to my earlier *From the Ghetto to the Main: The Story of the Jews of Montreal*, was so enthusiastic, that I felt another book would meet a real hunger for memories of the Montreal Jewish past.

Thus, in part, it stems from the interest in the nostalgic re-creation of those fabulous years growing up in Jewish Montreal. And, with regret, I feel we are talking about a past gone beyond recall—except in books like this.

When a croupier in Las Vegas writes me for a copy of *Ghetto* and asks plaintively, "Do you know anyone coming this way who could bring me some Montreal bagels?", I feel in touch with my reading public.

I also find it significant that, in my endless trek to used book sales, I have never found a copy of *Ghetto*. It is one of those books that remains on the shelf, to be consulted periodically—with chuckles at the memories it inspires.

The Copy Editor for *Baron Byng to Bagels: Tales of Jewish Montreal*—Heather Solomon-Bowden—said she couldn't put the book down. I explained that was because I had put glue on the cover.

Joe King—(Jewish) Montreal—2006

Acknowledgements

The author wishes to express his appreciation to the following for their assistance in researching this book, and the extraordinary collection of illustrations therein:

Janice Rosen and Helen Vallee, Canadian Jewish Congress, National Archives, Montreal
Shannon Hodge and Eiran Harris, Jewish Public Library, Montreal
National Library and Archives of Canada, Ottawa
Ottawa Civic Library
Toronto Reference Library
McGill University Libraries

and the following Montreal-area Public Libraries
- Atwater Library
- Bibliothèque nationale du Québec
- Eleanor London Cote St. Luc Library
- Fraser-Hickson Institute
- Reginald J.P. Dawson Town of Mount Royal Library
- Westmount Library

The Montreal Jewish Publication Society
expresses its deep appreciation to the following supporters who helped make this book possible:

Grand Patrons

Mildred Lande, C.M.
Judge Barbara Seal, C.M. and
Donald Seal, Q.C.

Patrons

Hillel Becker
Hon. Lawrence Bergman, N.A.
Rosalind and Morris Goodman
Steffi Halton
Sandra and Leo Kolber Foundation
Lewis C. Smith Foundation
Ben Weider

Sponsors

Alexander Meyers
Dorothy Reitman, C.M.
Norman Spector
Synagogue Council of Greater Montreal
Women's Federation CJA

Benefactors

David Azrieli
Prof. Lawrence M. Bessner, FCA
Canada-Israel Securities
Canadian Hadassah-WIZO
Federation CJA
Leonard Ellen Family Foundation
Hebrew Free Loan
Hon. Sheila Finestone
Kappy Flanders
Thomas Otto Hecht
Jewish Rehabilitation Hospital
Sheila and Marvyn Kussner
Maisliner
Drs. Maxine and Harvey Sigman
Dr. Louis Z.G. Touyz
Merle Wolofsky

Supporters

Ruth and Manuel G. Batshaw
Dale Boidman
Marcel Braitstein
Rita Briansky
Morley M. and Rita Cohen Foundation
Jack Dym
Rosetta Elkin
Dr. Phil Gold
Hebrew Free Loan
Prof. Fred Lowy
Norman Jaskolka, FCA
Robert Libman
Mr. Justice Herbert Marx
Greta Matus
Montreal Hadassah-WIZO
Soryl and Gerald Soiferman
Edward Wolkove, C.A.

Part One

A Chronological History of Jewish Montreal

A Chronological History of Jewish Montreal

1608 - The first historian of New France, Marc Lescarbot, writes numerous passages in Hebrew, and demonstrates a remarkable familiarity with the Hebrew language, the Talmud and Jewish history. Lescarbot seeks, in vain, for evidence that Canadian Indians are descended from the Ten Lost Tribes of Israel.

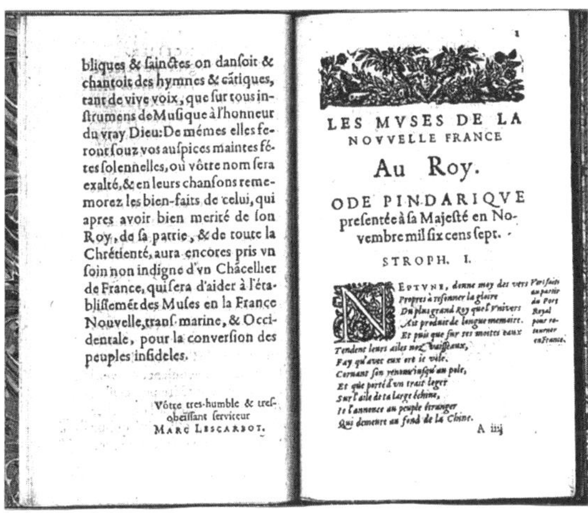

bliques & ſainctes on danſoit & chantoit des hymnes & cātiques, tant de vive voix, que ſur tous inſtrumens de Muſique à l'honneur du vray Dieu: De mémes elles feront ſouz vos auſpices maintes fétes ſolennelles, où vôtre nom ſera exalté, & en leurs chanſons rememorez les bien-faits de celui, qui apres avoir bien merité de ſon Roy, de ſa patrie, & de toute la Chrétienté, aura encores pris vn ſoin non indigne d'vn Chācellier de France, qui ſera d'aider à l'établiſſemēt des Muſes en la France Nouvelle, tranſ-marine, & Occidentale, pour la converſion des peuples infideles.

Vôtre tres-humble & tres-obeiſſant ſerviteur
MARC LESCARBOT.

1

LES MVSES DE LA NOVVELLE FRANCE

Au Roy.

ODE PINDARIQVE presentée à ſa Majeſté en Novembre mil ſix cens ſept.

STROPH. I.

NEPTVNE, donne moy des vers
Propres à reſonner la gloire
Du plus grand Roy que l'Vnivers
Ait produit de longue memoire.
Et puis que ſur tes moites eaux
Tendent leurs ailes noz vaiſſeaux,
Fay qu'avec eux ore je vole.
Cernant ſon renom juſqu'au pole,
Et que porté d'vn trait leger
Sur l'aile de ta large échine,
Je l'annonce au peuple étranger
Qui demeure au fond de la Chine.

Vers faits au partir du Port Royal pour retourner en France.

A iij

Historian Marc Lescarbot wrote passages of his 1608 history of New France in Hebrew.

The Eighteenth Century

1738 - A young Jewish woman, Esther Brandeau, becomes the first Jew, in official records, to set foot in New France where residence is denied to all but Roman Catholics. Brandeau, calling herself Jacques La Fargue, had travelled dressed as a man. The nuns hurriedly sewed "appropriate" clothing for her and clerics spent a year in an effort to convert her. When she finally made it clear she would not give up her faith, the young woman is returned to France, at the personal expense of King Louis XV. Quite possibly, Brandeau had made the hazardous journey to rejoin a (secretly Jewish) boyfriend.

Records show that a number of Jews sailed for New France but were intercepted and taken to Louisbourg, Nova Scotia, where they underwent conversion.

In 1740, George Hart, a Jew from New England, moved to Quebec and married a Roman Catholic girl.

Nevertheless, there were unconverted Jews living in the Royal Colony, to whom officials turned a blind eye. For example, Joseph de Silva, referred to as the "so-called Portuguese," was a creditor of the Colonial government.

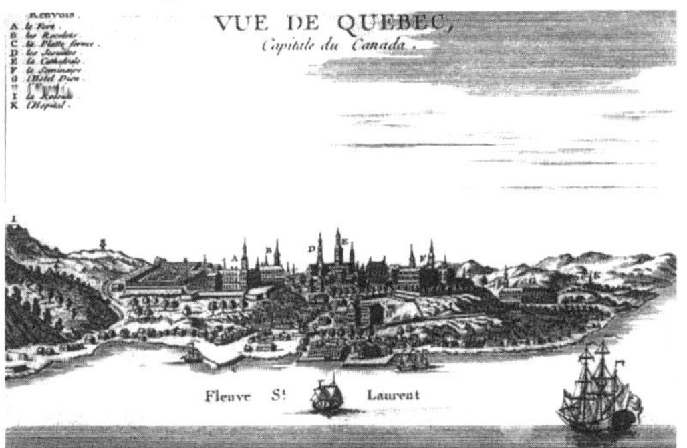

An impression of Quebec City at the time when Esther Brandeau stepped ashore there, disguised as a man.

And a number of other Sephardic Jewish names appear, including Toledano, Valenis, Maranda (a possible distortion of Miranda), Joseph Coste (probably corrupted from Costa), and Amereydos.

Map of Bordeaux, France, in the mid-18th Century showing the extensive Jewish Quarter, where the Gradis family lived.

1744 - Abraham Gradis, a prominent Jewish merchant of Bordeaux, sends his ship, the Fort Louis, to Quebec.

The Gradis family were prominent bankers and shipbuilders and were of immense service to France, grateful that they had been allowed to take refuge there from Spain. David Gradis founded the House of Gradis merchant bankers in 1696, and the company was among the creators of the French merchant marine. They also repeatedly rescued the colony of New France from starvation. In the middle of the 18th Century, the family sent 17 shiploads of supplies to Canada and French Caribbean colonies.

In 1748, Abraham Gradis—David's eldest son—founded the Society of Canada, seeking to strengthen trading ties between the colony and the mother country.

The French military commander in New France, at this time, General Montcalm, often paid tribute to the Jewish family and entrusted his correspondence to them rather than to French officials. The General, writing his mother, the Marquise Saint Veran, in 1757, noted, "M. de la Porte, is so neglectful, that I must ask you not to write through him anymore, but through M. Gradis at Bordeaux."French historian Camille Julian wrote that the Gradis family did more for the protection of French interests in Canada than "royalty itself." Paris neglected the colony; Montcalm noted at another time that the starving population had begun "to eat grass and herbs."

Captain (later Sir) Alexander Schomberg, a major figure in the conquest of New France.

1759 - British forces, under the command of General James Wolfe, defeat Montcalm on the Plains of Abraham. One of his major advisors was Captain (later Sir) Alexander Schomberg, commander of the frigate Diane. Schomberg was repeatedly recognized as an important figure in the campaign. Wolfe wrote four pages in the naval officers' diary on his plans for capturing New France, and even drew a map in pencil. The

The British attack on Quebec City, with Alexander Schomberg chosen by General Wolfe to command the first wave of attackers. (National Archives of Canada C 788)

Jewish officer was chosen to lead the first (red) wave of attackers on the day of the final battle. And Schomberg was given the honour of carrying word of the British victory to the King in London.

Jewish names appear in some military records of 1759 and 1760. A soldier named Abraham was taken prisoner in November 1759. He was part of a detachment carrying dispatches from Crown Point to General Wolfe at Quebec City. Other records show that Jacob Wolf and Joseph Wexler re-enlisted in the Second Battalion of the Royal American Regiment at Quebec City.

General François de Lévy, whose family crest bore three stars of David.

1760 - French General François de Lévy, of Jewish descent, leads a rag-tag French army from Montreal and defeats the British at Quebec City. However, at the moment of triumph, two sails were spotted in the St. Lawrence River. They proved to be British naval craft—Alexander Schomberg's Diana, and the Vanguard. They swept up the river and destroyed Lévy's transports, with all his supplies. The bitter French general was forced to withdraw to Montreal, abandoning his wounded and his cannon. There, under orders, he reluctantly surrendered to the British.

It is claimed that de Lévy's family descended from the Hebrew tribe of Levi. The city of Lévis is named in his honour and Pointe de Lévy is named after another member of his family.

1760 - Britain's General Sir Jeffrey Amherst rode, victorious, into Montreal, with Aaron Hart at his side. Hart became the first official Jewish resident of Canada, settling in Trois-Rivières where he became an important fur trader and property owner. Also in the ranks of those entering Montreal, with Amherst, were Emanuel de Cordova, Hananiel Garcia and Isaac Miranda.

Governor Haldimand wrote in the summer of 1764 that "the group of British merchants in Trois-Rivières was "composed of a Jew and of a sergeant and an Irish soldier on half pay."

THE
FORM
OF
PRAYER,
Which was performed at the
JEWS Synagogue,
IN THE
City of *NEW-YORK*,
On Thursday *October* 23, 1760;
Being the Day appointed by Proclamation for a General Thanksgiving to Almighty GOD, for the Reducing of *Canada* to His Majesty's Dominions.
Composed by D. R. JOSEPH YESURUN PINTO,
In the Hebrew Language:
And translated into English, by a Friend to Truth.

NEW-YORK:
Printed and Sold by W. WEYMAN, at his New Printing-Office, in Broad-Street, not far from the Exchange, 1760. (Price 4d.)
No. 39.

The Shearith Israel Congregation in New York celebrates the capture of Canada by the British.

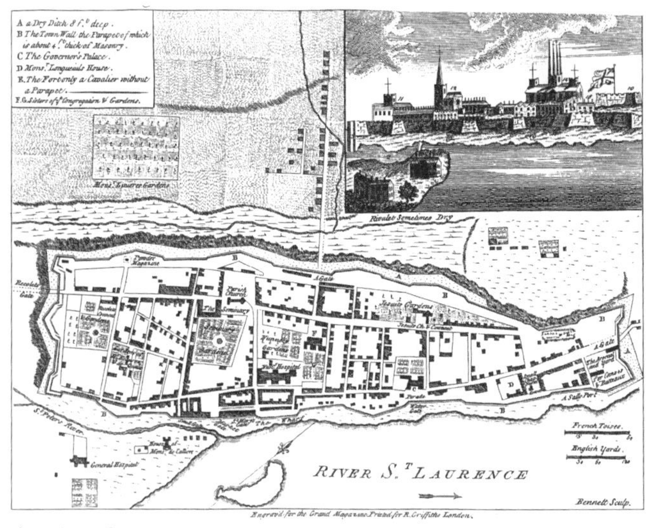

The city of Montreal as it looked in 1760 when the first Jews—mostly merchants—arrived.

1761-1763 - The first Jewish settlers in Montreal, Trois-Rivières and Quebec (the three major population centres at this time): Aaron and Moses Hart; Samuel Judah; Abraham, Jacob and David Salisbury Franks; Andrew Hays; Ezekiel, Levy and Meyer Solomons; Manuel Gomez; Eleazor, Gershon, Isaac and Simon Levy; David Lazarus; Meyer Michaels; Fernandez de Fonseca; Hananiel Garcia; Jacob de Maurera; Andrew Hays; Isaac, Joseph, Samuel and Uriah Judah; Barnet Lyons, Joseph Bindona; Chapman Andrews; Elias Salomon, Hyam Myers, Pines Heineman; Samuel Jacobs, Elias Seixas, and Emanuel de Cordova. (This list was developed from commercial and military documents. Not all of these pioneers stayed. Many returned to such places as New York and Philadelphia. One major reason: a scarcity of Jewish women.)

1763 - Montreal Jews pay the ransom to free Ezekiel Solomons. He had been taken captive by Indians near his trading post in Michilimackinac. His partners were Levy Solomons (probably a cousin), Chapman Abraham, Benjamin Lyon and Gershon Levy. He was fortunate to escape alive. On another occasion, renegade French soldiers and Indians slaughtered a British garrison.

1764 - The first Jewish child, David David, is born in Montreal. He becomes an important landowner, and a major figure in philanthropy.

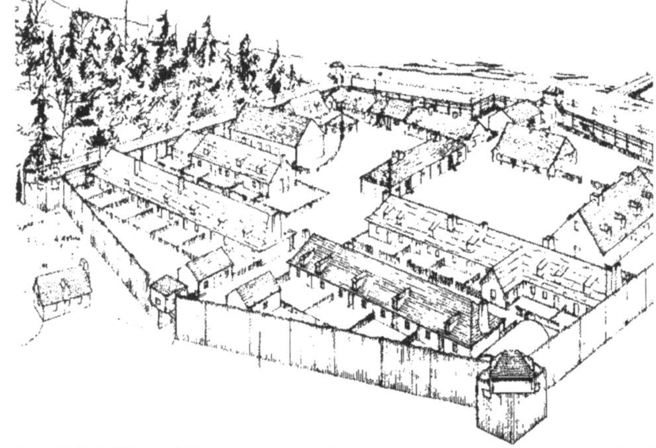

Fort Michilimackinac was at the centre of lawlessness which saw the kidnapping and ransoming of Montrealer Ezekiel Solomons.

David David, the first Jewish child born in Montreal.

David started off working with the North West Company, travelling by canoe into the Canadian wilds to trade for furs. He became sufficiently prominent that, in 1817, he was admitted to Montreal's prestigious Beaver Club. (Other Jewish members of the Club included Myer Michaels and Samuel David.)

From 1818 to 1824, he was a Director of the Bank of Montreal. He was also a member of the committee promoting construction of the Lachine Canal and the Canal's board. A lifelong bachelor, he became one of the largest property owners in Montreal. He developed a large fur trading business, with partners, including his brothers Moses and Samuel, and his brothers-in-law, Myer Michaels and Andrew Hays. They set up trading posts in such places as York (the future Toronto) and the Detroit area. Ultimately, the business was sold to the North West Company.

On his death, David David's estate was valued at £70,000—an immense sum at that time.

1767 - Lazarus David (father of David David) and Simon Levy become the first Jewish landowners of record in Montreal.

1768 - Congregation Shearith Israel (later the Spanish and Portuguese) is founded in Montreal—the fourth Jewish congregation in North America. The others, all Sephardic, are in New York City, Philadelphia and Charleston, South Carolina.

The first few families met in each other's homes until the Congregation was formally established, in 1777.

The first, tiny synagogue was built at the corner of Little St. James Street and Notre Dame.

1775 - Montreal is captured by American Revolutionary Forces and for part of that 188-day occupation, Moses Hazen is Military Governor of the city. When the Americans are forced to retreat, Hazen has to flee with the 2nd Canadian Regiment he recruited. He later became a Brigadier General in the Revolutionary Army and his Regiment, largely French Canadian, fought for the Americans and received land grants.

American Revolutionary forces capture Montreal and hold the city for 188 days.

1775 - Lazarus David purchases land on St. Janvier Street (now Dominion Square) to serve "in perpetuity as a cemetery for individuals of the Jewish faith who may die in the Montreal district." David himself becomes the first person to be buried there.

1777 - Shearith Israel builds Canada's first synagogue, at the corner of Notre Dame and St. James, on land provided by David David.

Jewish Loyalists from America settled in Quebec's Eastern Townships. Americans loyal to the British Crown flooded into Canada and other British colonies after the Revolution.

1777 - Jacob Kuhn is named Bailiff of Montreal and holds that position, according to documents, for at least 10 years. Later, he assumed a position which today would be called Police Commissioner.

The Nineteenth Century

1801 - Henry Joseph inaugurates the first direct marine service between Canada and England with his vessel the "Eweretta." He is regarded as the founder of Canada's merchant marine.

1806 - Members of the Jewish community join in the celebration at "Hamilton's" of Nelson's victory at Trafalgar.

1807 - Aaron Hart's son, Ezekiel, is elected member for Trois-Rivières in the Legislative Assembly of Lower Canada, but is refused the right to take his seat—not because he is Jewish—but because it is felt he will vote with the English.

1812 - Jewish officers in the War of 1812 include three Hart brothers—Moses, Ezekiel and Benjamin; Lieut. Col. Samuel David; Captain David David, Lieutenant Moses David; Jacob and Benjamin Franks, and Henry Joseph. Out of a population of about 100, at this time, three Jews served as Colonels, and 10 or more others were officers.

1818 - Charter members of the Bank of Montreal include Henry Joseph, Moses Judah Hays and David David. David David is elected a director.

1819 *- The Jewish "merchants and traders" of Montreal listed in a booklet prepared that year by Thomas Doige (price 5 shillings) : David David, merchant, 14 Notre Dame Street. Samuel David, Merchant, 1, Place d'Armes, DH 103,*

Nelson's Monument in Montreal; stones for the monument were transported aboard Henry Joseph's "Eweretta." Joseph was the father of Canada's merchant marine. (W.H. Bartlett engraving)

33.d If any Despute should arise between any Members of the Congregation they shall be obliged to come before the Mahamad that they may Endeavour to settle it before they go to any Magistrate or be liable to such a Penalty as they may think proper

34.th No Person to be admitted without the Consent of the Junto ——

35th All Monies Expended by the Parnasses during their Acting out of their own Capital shall be made good - by those who are Chosen to Succeed them

36.th The Shamas shall be obliged to Carry each Member his Account

37.th The Gabay shall lay before the Junto the Monies Expended & Received During his Acting. the Week before Rosh Hashanah

38.th The Parnass is not to lay out any Money for the Congregation without the Consent of the Majority of the Adjuntos

We the Underwritten do hereby most Solemnly Promise in the Name of the Almighty God to abide by the above Regulations, or to be Liable to such Restrictions as is herein Specified. as Witness our Hands the 3d day of our Month Tebeth 5539 1778

Levy Solomons Parnass
Uriah Judah — Gabay

Samuel Judah
Andrew Hays
[illegible]
Hyam Michaels
Abm. Franks
Myer Myers
David David
H: Heineman Pines
Barnet Lion
Abr. Judah
Sam David

A page from the 1778 minutes of the Spanish and Portuguese Synagogue. Note that the sixth signature is that of David David, the first Jew born in Montreal.

Ezekiel Hart.

De Salaberry leading Canadian forces, including a number of Jewish officers, in the 1813 Battle at Chateauguay.

The Bank of Montreal as it appeared to an artist in 1817.

Notre Dame Street, Montreal, 1830. (R.A. Sproul)

St. Antoine Street. Alexander Hart, Merchant, Craig Street, Counting-house, Fortification Lane. Benjamin Hart, Comission Merchant, 69, St. Paul Street—DH10, St. Urbain Street. Moses Hayes, Engineers Department, 15, St. Jacques Street. Jacob Franks, Fur Merchant, 2, St. Charles Barommee Street. John Levi, Dry Goods Merchant, 43, St, Paul Street. Mrs. Levy, Tavern Keeper, 6, Old Market Place. Levi and Benjamin S. Solomons & Co., Tobacconists and Chocolate Manufacturers, 41, St. Paul Street. Benjamin Solomons, Tobacconist, Dh. 5, St. Sacrement Street. Henry Solomons, Furrier, 138, St. Paul Street.

1829 - The Legislature of Lower Canada approves a petition creating a Jewish religious corporation, with power for its "ministers to celebrate marriages, and keep registers of births, marriages and deaths."

1830 - Aaron Philip Hart becomes the first Jewish lawyer in Canada.

1831 - The Jewish population of Canada is 107.

1832 - The Legislature of Lower Canada passes a bill declaring that all persons professing the Jewish religion are entitled to the full rights and privileges of other subjects of His Majesty. This is the first declaration of equality in the British Empire. (It was 1858, 26 years later, before Jews could take office in the British Government, without, at least nominally, converting.)

1832 - Arthur Wellington Hart, a grandson of Aaron Hart of Trois-Rivières, becomes the first Jew to settle in Toronto. Toronto (then known as York) had a population of 9,000. Hart, apparently representing his grandfather's wholesale mercantile house and the Eagle Life Assurance Company of

Montreal in 1827.

London, rented a two-storey facility on King Street, then the main commercial street of the town.

1832 - Moses Judah Hayes installed Montreal's first municipal water system. Until then, householders rolled barrels down to the river for their water supply, or depended on primitive, uncertain supply through pipes. The water works were the pride of the small city.

MONTREAL Judicial Archives

Register to remain of Record in the Prothonotaries Office for the District of Montreal wherein persons residing in the said District being British subjects and professing the Jewish Religion, being above the age of twenty one Years, may, under and by Virtue of the Provincial Statute 9 & 10 George IV. chapter 75, inscribe their names, ages, additions and places of residence.

(1829) Monk & Morrogh P.B.R.

Oath to be taken in conformity with the said Statute.

I A.B. do swear that I believe myself to be of the full age of twenty one years and that I am a British subject professing the Jewish faith,

1 Henry Joseph Senior 55 years Merchant Berthier
2 Alex^r Hart 48 years Gentleman Montreal
3 Benjamin Hart 51 years Merchant ditto
4 Isaac Valentine 40 Years Gentleman Montreal
5 M. J. Hays 32 Years Gentleman Do
6 H. Solomon 42 " Furrier Do
7 M. Levy 28 Do Do
8 Samuel David 40 Do Do
9 [illegible] Hart 62 Merchant Do
10 Esdaile P. Cohen 32 Merchant Do
11 Jacob Jacobs 33 Merchant Montreal
12 Isaac Aaron 39 Montreal Merchant
13 Saml Joseph 29 Merchant Berthier
14 D. C. David 21 Student at Law Montreal
15 A. R. Hart 21 and over Advocate
16 A. H. David 35 Physician
17 Jacob H. Joseph 22 Merchant
18 Samuel Hart 21 do
19 Theodore Hart 21 do
20 Henry Bernstein 47 years Teacher Montreal
21 Moses Samuel David 21 years Gentleman "
22 David Piza 22 years Minister "
23 Jesse Joseph 22 years Merchant Montreal
Myer Solomons 23 years Student Montreal
25 Lewis Lyons 42 years Merchant Montreal
26 Davidson A Philipps 37 years Merchant Montreal
27 [illegible] 31 years Trader Montreal

A list of Montreal Jews from 1829. They registered and took the oath of loyalty to King George IV.

Moses Judah Hayes erected Montreal's first municipal water works system.

The Chenneville Synagogue as engraved in 1839.

PROVINCIAL STATUTES

OF

LOWER-CANADA.

Anno Regni Primo Gulielmi IV.

HIS EXCELLENCY

MATTHEW LORD AYLMER, K. C. B.

GOVERNOR IN CHIEF.

Preamble.

WHEREAS doubts have arisen whether persons professing the Jewish Religion are by law entitled to many of the privileges enjoyed by the other subjects of His Majesty within this Province: Be it therefore declared and enacted by the King's Most Excellent Majesty, by and with the advice and consent of the Legislative Council and Assembly of the Province of Lower Canada, constituted and assembled by virtue of and under the authority of an Act passed in the Parliament of Great Britain, intituled, "An Act to repeal certain parts of an Act passed in "the fourteenth year of His Majesty's Reign, intituled, "*An Act for making* "*more effectual provision for the Government of the Province of Quebec, in North* "*America,*" and to make further provision for the Government of the said "Province of Quebec in North America;" And it is hereby declared and enacted by the authority aforesaid, that all persons professing the Jewish Religion being natural born British subjects inhabiting and residing in this Province, are entitled and shall be deemed, adjudged and taken to be entitled to the full rights and privileges of the other subjects of His Majesty, his Heirs or Successors, to all intents, constructions and purposes whatsoever, and capable of taking, having or enjoying any office or place of trust whatsoever, within this Province.

Persons professing the Jewish Religion to be entitled to all the civil rights of British Subjects.

The Declaration giving Jews equal rights in Quebec.

Jews on the Register of British Subjects in 1832:

Name:	Age:	Occupation:
Henry Joseph Senior	55	Merchant
Alexander Hart	48	Gentleman
Benjamin Hart	51	Merchant
Isaac Valentine	43	Gentleman
M.J. Hays	32	Gentleman
H. Solomon	42	Furrier
M. Davis	28	Furrier
Samuel Davis	40	Furrier
M. Hart	62	Merchant
Esdaile P. Cohen	32	Merchant
Jacob Jacobs	33	Merchant
Isaac Aaron	39	Merchant
Samuel Joseph	29	Merchant
E.D. David	21	Student-at-law
A.P. Hart	21 and +	Advocate
A.H. David	25	Physician
Jacob H. Joseph	22	Merchant
Samuel Hart	21	Merchant
Theodore Hart	21	Merchant
Henry Bernstein	47	Teacher
Moses Samuel David	81	Gentleman
David Piza	22	Minister (Rabbi)

Canada's first locomotive; the Joseph Family helped make the first railway a reality.

1834 - Dr. Aaron David Hart is the first Canadian-born Jew to practise medicine in Canada.

1835 - Frank N. Hart is the first Jew to graduate from McGill College with a medical degree.

1835 - Land is purchased on Chenneville Street for a synagogue. The biggest contribution, 575 pounds, comes from David David's sister, Mrs. Frances Michaels.

1837 - Rebellions break out in Lower Canada (Quebec) and Upper Canada (Ontario) and Jews, generally, remain loyal to the crown. During the Battle of St. Charles (Nov. 25), Captain Eleazor David, commanding the cavalry, has his horse shot from under him, but escapes serious injury. He is mentioned in dispatches and is promoted, by Sir John Colborne, to the rank of Major.

1840 - General and Lady Clitherton attend services at the Shearith Israel Synagogue.

1841 - The Jewish population of Canada reaches 154.

1845 - Moses Judah Hayes is appointed Chief of Police for Montreal. He holds the post until his death, in 1861.

Moses Judah Hayes was an outstanding citizen of Montreal—in the tiny Jewish community, and in the general one. Hayes, who was an engineer, installed steam pumping engines to draw water from the St. Lawrence River for his Montreal Water Works. The old wooden pipes were dug up and replaced

1836 - The Champlain and St. Lawrence Railway, the first Canadian Railway, begins operations. It was constructed by Jacob and Jesse Joseph.

CHAMPLAIN & SAINT LAWRENCE

RAIL-ROAD.

NEW ARRANGEMENT.

UNTIL further Notice, the Hours of departure will be :—

STEAMERS.

From Montreal.	*From Laprairie.*
7 o'clock, A. M.	6¼ o'clock, A. M.
12 o'clock, Noon, U. S. Mail & Passengers	9¼ o'clock, A. M.
4 o'clock, P. M.	2 o'clock, P. M.
	5¼ o'clock, P. M.

RAIL-ROAD CARS.

From St. Johns.	*From Laprairie.*
8¼ o'clock, A. M.	9¼ o'clock, A. M.
12 o'clock, Noon.	1¼ o'clock, P. M.
4 o'clock, P. M.	5¼ o'clock, P. M.

A. H. BRAINERD,
Superintendent.

Montreal, October 18, 1849. 169

Montreal in 1840. Merchants, including Jewish traders, moved a lot of their goods by raft.

with four-inch iron pipes. The Water Works were the pride of Montreal. Rev. Newton Bosworth wrote in 1839 "Montreal is better supplied with water than any other city on this continent, with the exception of Philadelphia."After selling the installation to the city, he constructed the massive Hayes Block, 1846-1847, with splendid shops at the lower level, a hotel on the second floor and the large Hayes Theatre in the back.

However, in 1852, the entire block was destroyed by fire.

The penniless Hayes was given the job of police chief to provide him with a living. It was not an easy job. The City budgeted less than a dollar a day for police officers and Hayes often had to recruit his constables from among prisoners jailed for the night for being drunk and disorderly. On his death, in 1861, the Montreal Gazette *wrote: "As a merchant, private citizen, and public officer, Mr. Hayes had gained the esteem of all classes."*

1846 - The Congregation of English, German and Polish Jews (later called the Congregation Shaar Hashomayim) is established—-Canada's first Ashkenazi Congregation.

1847 - The Hebrew Philanthropic Society is founded with Moses Judah Hayes as President. It assists 39 people in its first year, at a total cost of $111.

1848 - Rabbi Abraham de Sola is appointed lecturer in Hebrew and Oriental Literature at McGill University. He becomes a full professor in 1853

The great fire of 1852. Dalhousie Square and Hayes' House go up in flames (by James Duncan, The Illustrated London News*)*

Steamboat wharf, Montreal, 1849. (James Duncan lithograph)

1851 - The census shows 351 Jews living in Canada—181 in Montreal, 40 in Quebec and 77 in Toronto.

1857 - Immigrant Jews from Russia and Lithuania, including Noah Friedman, the Kellerts, William Jacobs, and others, settle in the Lancaster, Ont., area but later move to Montreal. In 1858, Alexander Vineberg becomes the first Jew to live in Cornwall, but later the family moves to Montreal.

In that same year, Moses Bilsky arrived in Ottawa. He is believed to be the first Jew to settle in the capital city area. With formation of the first synagogue in Toronto (a rented room over a chemist's shop at the corner of Richmond and Yonge Streets), Mr. and Mrs. G.I. Ascher of Montreal presented the new congregation with a Sefer Torah. Many of those who settled in Toronto had moved there from Montreal.

An 1856 engraving of the Mechanics Institute, Montreal's first library. Many Jews studied here in what became the Atwater Library

1858 - Abraham Joseph is involved in the founding of the Banque Nationale.

1861 - Samuel Davis establishes the first cigar factory in Montreal.

1862 - Isaac Singer invents his famous sewing machine. Jews, in particular, utilize the new invention. Jews introduce the manufacture of ready-made clothing to Canada. In time, it will become the largest industry in Montreal.

The Jewish tailor shop was the modest beginning but, as the years went by, the industry gradually grew into a massive employer—providing jobs for thousands of Jews, and later, thousands of Montrealers.

L.L. Levy led the effort to establish a Hebrew Benefit Society that met on Great St. James Street West.

1863 - L.L. Levy invites Jewish bachelors to attend a meeting "above Mr. Wright's store, on Great St. James Street," to consider the desirability of forming an organization to assist "needy or unfortunate co-religionists." The Young Men's Hebrew Benevolent Society is organized "under the supervision and control of the young unmarried men of the city."

1870 - Dr. Aaron David Hart is appointed the Dean of the Faculty of Medicine at Bishop's College.

1870 - During the Fenian Raids, Captain David A. Hart commanded the First Prince of Wales Rifles. He was involved in a number of major actions.

1871 - The Quebec Jewish population is 518.

1871 - A Jewish electrical engineer, Sigismund Mohr, arrives in Quebec from his native Germany. He developed the first hydro-power in Canada and introduced the first telephone and electric light systems. He harnessed the Montmorency Falls, bringing electricity to Quebec City in 1885, Sherbrooke, a year later, and Montreal in 1898.

List of Jews aged 21 and over, in 1874, who have "taken the oath and are British subjects":

Name	Age	Occupation
Meldola de Sola	21	*Broker and Commission Merchant*
Lyon Silverman	30	*Jeweller*
Levi Abrahams	34	*Tobacconist*
Morris Teichman	54	*Tavern-keeper*
M. Sternberg	26	*Merchant*
J. Sternberg	23	*Merchant*
W.B. Garcia	29	*Merchant*
Israel Rubenstein	28	*Silver Plater*
A. Edward Cohen	33	*Merchant*
Sullivan David	29	*Merchant*
Joseph Moss	29	*Merchant*
Jacob E. Moss	31	*Merchant*

1875-1877 - The first English and Hebrew Day School is established by the English, German and Polish Congregation (Shaar Hashomayim) in Montreal.

1880 - The Montefiore Club is founded.

1881 - The first B'nai Brith Lodge is established in Montreal.

1881 - Quebec Jewish population, 989.

1882 - The Jewish population of Montreal more than doubles as thousands of Jews flee Russian pogroms.

Between 1880 and 1917, some 2,000,000 Jews flee the Russian Empire. About 30,000 came to Canada and most chose to settle in Montreal.

1882 - The first Reform Congregation in Canada, Temple Emanu-El, is founded.

1884 - Jesse Joseph is named President of the Montreal Street Railway Company. Three years later, he becomes President of the Montreal Gas Company. (A lifelong bachelor, he lives to be 86 and has a mansion where the McGill University McLennan Library is today. His estate, at the corner of what is now Sherbrooke Street and McTavish, was so large he had cows grazing on the lawns to supply fresh milk to his household). Joseph pioneered commercial relations between Canada and Belgium, and he served, for more than 40 years, as the Belgian Consul in Montreal. Belgium honoured him twice for his services—naming him a Chevalier of the Order

The Montreal waterfront in 1875.
(Canadian Illustrated News)

The Montreal fish market in 1880. A number of Jewish fishmongers did business here.

Jesse Joseph's Mansion, "Dilcoosha" (Hindustani word meaning "Heart's Delight"). The mansion was built on the corner of Sherbrooke and McTavish Streets.

Ekiel Bronfman and his family settle, in 1889, on a farm near Wapella, Saskatchewan.

of Leopold and, later, he was awarded the Decoration Civique of the First Class.

When Jesse Joseph died, in 1904, aged 86, the Montreal Star *commented: "Montreal loses a citizen who has for years held a prominent position among her financiers and merchant princes, and one who will be long remembered for his talent displayed in the organization and direction of great public undertakings."*

He was, by far, the richest Jew in Montreal at that time, and lived in considerable luxury.

1886 - The Spanish and Portuguese Congregation opens English and Hebrew Day School classes.

1886 - Destitute Jewish refugees in their thousands overwhelm the Jewish Community, which explodes from 1,000 to 5,000. The entire community, under the leadership of Bishop William Bond, holds an emergency mass meeting and three warehouses, on St. Peter Street, are converted into dormitories and dining halls for the new arrivals.

1890 - With the arrival of a large number of destitute Jews, the situation became so critical in Montreal that Joseph Goldstein, Treasurer of the Young Men's Hebrew Benevolent Society, writes the Austrian Jewish philanthropist, Baron Maurice de Hirsch, asking urgently for assistance. Hirsch sends $20,000 and wrote Society President Harris Vineberg that "more funds are available if required." More Russian Jews sought sanctuary in Montreal than in New York!

1891 - A large store at 7 St. Elizabeth Street is renovated and officially opened, on June 17, as "The Baron de Hirsch Institute."

1896 - Rabbi M. Ashinsky founds the first Talmud Torah in Canada.

1896 - Regina L. Landau is the first Jewish woman doctor in Canada, graduating from Bishop's College. She practised, for a time, in Montreal.

1899 - 3,000 Jewish immigrants, mostly from Romania, arrive in Montreal.

The Baron de Hirsch, after the death of his only son, increasingly devoted his life and fortune to assisting Jews in distress worldwide.

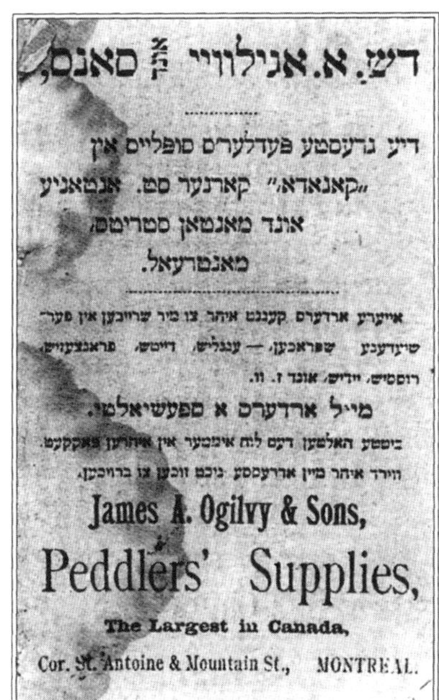

James A. Ogilvy & Sons of Montreal advertise, in Yiddish, in 1897 to encourage Jewish peddlers to obtain their supplies from them. (Canadian Jewish Congress National Archives Montreal)

Rebecca of Montreal

The heroine of Sir Walter Scott's famous novel, *Ivanhoe,* had a Montreal connection. The original for the fictional Rebecca was Rebecca Gratz of Philadelphia. Montreal Jewish pioneer Henry Joseph would proudly show off Thomas Sully's painting of Rebecca. Joseph had married Rebecca's niece, Sara Moses, in 1848. When Sara's parents had both died young, her aunt—who never married—had raised her and, after her marriage, would visit Montreal. But before she would allow her niece to marry, Rebecca had investigated and determined that the gentleman, Mr. Joseph of Canada, was a "young man of irreproachable character—a merchant in good business and respectable connections." Visiting Montreal, the Philadelphia grand dame found Montreal to be "almost medieval with narrow streets, imperfect pavements and low stone houses." With the prevalence of French, she felt she was in a foreign country. But, after a time, she described the city as "lying on the bosom of the noble St. Lawrence" and said the city made a "fine impression."

The strange thing is that while Sir Walter Scott accurately described Rebecca in his novel, he never met her!

Scott learned about Rebecca Gratz from a member of her Philadelphia circle, author Washington Irving. When Scott told Irving he was thinking of putting a female Jewish character in his new book, he enthusiastically described his Philadelphia friend—her talents, her loveliness, her many kindnesses. Scott became excited and exclaimed, "You have given me my Rebecca."

Clarence de Sola became the first President of the Canadian Zionist Organization

THE TWENTIETH CENTURY

1900 - The First Canadian Zionist Convention is held in Montreal.

1900 - The Baroness de Hirsch dies in Paris, leaving a bequest of $89,000 (600,000 francs). This prompted a change of the organization's name to "The Baron de Hirsch Institute and Hebrew Benevolent Society."

Hersch Wolofsky, future publisher of the Kanader Adler *(the Montreal Yiddish newspaper), wrote—in his autobiography— of how the poor were helped circa 1900 by the "machers" of the Baron de Hirsch Institute: "The pioneer philanthropists, in their wisdom, saw fit to adopt the wicker technique of a bank—five dollar bills in one pile, two dollar bills in another, and silver neatly heaped up according to denomination. The needy would come thus to the dispensers of charity, and explain their difficulties. Then and there the decision would be made, and a five dollar bill would be taken off one pile, or a quarter off the other, the whole depending upon the persuasiveness of the petitioner and the sensitivity of the cashier." Often it was only the women, with hungry children, who would ask for help. The men would feel too humiliated to ask.*

The Baroness de Hirsch

1901 - Quebec's Jewish population stands at 7,607.

"Meat sold for six cents a pound...A spring chicken could be bought for a quarter, two for forty-five cents. Fish was not purchased; one went down to the river-front, every Wednesday and Thursday, fish still struggling in groups upon their strings. Rent was also comparatively cheap, four and five room flats renting from eight to ten dollars a month."—Hersh Wolofsky in his autobiography

1902 - The Jewish Endeavour Sewing School is organized to block efforts to convert Jewish girls.

In addition to sewing, the girls are taught "honour, manners, cleanliness and neatness." One pupil, Minnie Cummings, met her future husband—Munroe Abbey (who was in a boxing class) at the School, and they became two of the most prominent leaders of the community, while their daughter, Sheila Abbey Finestone, became a Member of Parliament and then a Senator.

1905 - The first Yiddish Public Library in Canada is opened in Montreal, in a rented room.

1907 - A group of Jewish doctors, in cooperation with the Ladies Auxiliary of the King Edward Benefit Association, create the Herzl Dispensary.

The Herzl Dispensary—a step towards creating a Jewish hospital—is founded.

Housed at first at 832 St. Dominique Street, it was moved to larger facilities at 632 St. Urbain Street. A staff of 20 Jewish physicians treated 1,000 patients a month.

1907 - *The Kanader Adler (Jewish Daily Eagle)*, a daily Yiddish newspaper, is founded in Montreal.

1908 - The Jewish population of Montreal is estimated at 30,000.

1909 - The Young Men's Hebrew Association is formed. The first meetings are held in a small room in the Baron de Hirsch Institute on Sanguinet Street.

The treasurer, in the first months, often had to look for help to pay the $7.50 a month rent.

During one early financial crisis, with rent now $25, the Y had a bank balance of $15. The organization also needed furniture and equipment. Members, pressed for their help, contributed enough to pay the bills and make a down payment of $9 on furniture. The bank balance had shrunk to $1.

"The Montreal Jew is a self-supporting citizen and justly proud of it...A race that has no beggars, no drunkards, no prostitutes, no hoodlums, certainly has much to commend it."

—Oliver Asselin, The Jews of Montreal, *The Canadian Century, Sept. 16, 1911*

1909 - Herman Reitman, an immigrant from Romania who had been making a living selling from a pushcart, invests his savings in the formation of the "American Ladies' Tailoring and Dressmaking Company" on St. Lawrence Boulevard. Herman, his father and brother worked in the back of the shop, making coats and suits. It was the beginning of the enormous Reitman's chain. In 1926, they moved to Ste. Catherine Street opposite the Princess Theatre.

The "Main", St. Lawrence Boulevard, was an exotic enclave to neighbouring French Catholics and English Protestants, offering unique tastes, smells and sounds.

The original "Main" was confined to Lower St. Lawrence Boulevard (now known as Boulevard St-Laurent), below Sherbrooke Street. As the years rolled by, the Jewish community spread northward until—in the middle of the 20th Century—the Jewish Ghetto ran from Pine Avenue north to Bertrand Avenue, in the Mile End, with Park Avenue as the western boundary and St. Dominique representing the eastern limit. It was a fascinating place for non-Jews to visit, with its multitude of delis, barrels of pickles on the sidewalk, kosher butchers, bookstores and peddlers selling everything from used clothing and shoes to pots and pans, at bargain prices.

The peddlers, when they prospered, invested in a horse and wagon and patrolled the streets, noisily advertising their wares. Ultimately, many achieved the goal of opening a small corner store—often converting a room in their home.

A visit to the Main was an adventure, and non-Jews, hesitant at first because of the strange garb and language of the area, gradually began to shop there and experience such new treats as smoked meat and bagels.

In addition to bookstores and small lending libraries, every café was a meeting-place for friends who gathered to discuss an endless variety of topics. And when learning opportunities presented themselves, they took full advantage of them.

Montreal had few libraries, but they made use of the existing ones—the Mechanics Institute (later the Atwater Library) and the Fraser (later Fraser-Hickson Institute).

FLAT

TO LET

Apply To ______________

צו פארענטען

זיך ווענדען צו ______________

The Main was bilingual—English and Yiddish!

Novelist Hugh McLennan, wrote of the Main: "It was probably the most creative Jewish area in North America, more so even than New York, and out of it emerged men who became distinguished lawyers, businessmen (some on the grand scale) poets, novelists and musicians. In future years I was to discover that some of my dearest and most admired friends had grown up in this district.

The Main has been the most astonishing forcing house in Canada for culture and business."*

* avenue of opportunity

A. I. HAHAMOVITCH, Reg'd — Sole Distributors — 5182 ST. LAWRENCE BLVD.

CANADIAN JEWISH CHRONICLE

Canadian Jews "Doing Their Bit"

POSTER OF JEWISH OVERSEAS COMPANY

Jews recruit for the Great War—in Yiddish.

1911 - The Hebrew Free Loan is established in Montreal.

1911-1913 - Nearly 39,000 Jewish immigrants arrive in Montreal in a three-year span. They overwhelm the estimated community of 28,000.

In 1913, Montreal has 60,000 Jews; 30,000 live in Toronto and 20,000 in Winnipeg.

Many of the newcomers brought skills with them. They included carpenters, bakers, butchers, teachers, tailors, artisans, tinsmiths and tradesmen.

Half a century earlier, Isaac Singer had invented his familiar Singer Sewing Machine and approximately half the Jewish community found work in the steadily-expanding garment industry.

Immigrants would arrive, be met by friends or relatives on the waterfront and then walk, or be taken by horse and wagon (only the most prosperous) to sleep on the floor of their temporary accommodation. Quite possibly, the newcomer could go to work the next day—functioning in Yiddish—in a clothing factory. Almost the entire staff of the plant, from owner and foreman to workers, spoke Yiddish and the facilities closed for Jewish holidays. Much of the work was done at home, in their cold-water flats, with every member of the family, from eight years and up, helping. They earned as little as one or two dollars a week, clamped to their sewing machines 15 hours a day.

1912 - The Mount Sinai Sanitarium is created to provide free treatment for ailing immigrants.

1912 - Abraham Blumenthal is elected an alderman in Montreal.

1912 - The YMHA undertakes a membership drive, recruiting 1,260 members and becoming second only to New York in strength.

The horse market in 1915, located at the Bonsecours Market. A number of Jews were in the business of horse trading. And, in 1915, horses were still widely used.

1913 - Peretz School is founded in Montreal.

1914 - A Jewish library is formally founded, with a charter from Quebec, as a "library and a people's university." The library actually had been created in 1912, with modest quarters at 404 Main Street.

1914 - Jewish People's School opened in Montreal.

1914 - The wife of an immigrant rabbi, Toba Kaplan, urges the community to create a hospital for poor, pregnant women. Mrs. Kaplan, known as the "Greene Rebetzin", refused to allow her name to be put on a ward of the Hebrew Maternity Hospital when it became a reality.

1915-1918 - 4,700 Jews (out of a population of 12,417 21 and older) serve in the Canadian Expeditionary Force in World War I. 100 are killed in action; more than 80 are decorated for gallantry. Of 98 Jewish commissioned officers, the highest ranking were three Lieutenant-Colonels, Maurice Alexander, H.H. Lightstone and L. Lerner.

1916 - The Jewish Public Library begins operations at 669 St. Urbain Street.

1916 - The Federation of Jewish Philanthropies is incorporated. Its first campaign—two days in January during a blizzard—raises $127,000; that's $52,000 more than the same agencies raised the previous year.

The incorporators of the Federation:

Mortimer B. Davis	*Mark Workman*
Lyon Cohen	*Maxwell Goldstein,* K.C.*
Michael Hirsch	*D.S. Friedman*
S.W. Jacobs, K.C.*	*Clarence de Sola*
M.A. Vineberg	*J. Levinson*
J.A. Jacobs	*A.M. Vineberg*
Louis Lewis	*B. Goldstein*
S. Kellert	*Harris Vineberg*
H.M. Levine	*Rabbi Nathan Gordon*
Rabbi H. Abramowitz	*Dr. S. Vineberg*

* King's Counsel

1917 - King George V knights Mortimer B. Davis. He is the only Canadian Jew ever to be knighted.

Sir Mortimer found himself in a dilemma after a visit to New York, when he fell in love with a 17-year-old manicurist! What to do? A knight of the realm cannot marry a manicurist. The solution: he

Sir Mortimer B. Davis.

Lavy Becker played leadership roles in 25 Jewish community organizations, and helped found three different synagogues!

nominally married his lady friend to an Italian Count, for a $25,000 fee. A few months later, Sir Mortimer B. Davis married an Italian Countess!

1917 - Five Talmud Torahs unite under the name of United Talmud Torahs of Montreal.

1919 - The Jewish population of Montreal is estimated at 46,000.

1919 - Canadian Jewish Congress holds its first Plenary in Montreal.

1920 - The Jewish Immigrant Aid Society is established.

1921 - The first Hadassah Convention is held in Montreal.

1921 - Lavy Becker founds the Orthodox Young Israel Synagogue, then 30 years later he helps found Congregation Beth-El, and then, in 1960, he founds the Reconstructionist Synagogue, Dorshei Emet, and serves as its first Rabbi. Social worker, rabbi and, finally, an industrialist, Lavy Becker ultimately provides leadership, in Canada and internationally, to 25 Jewish organizations. He lives to be 95.

Two of the orphans rescued from Eastern Europe in 1921, by Harry Hershman of Montreal. (Canadian Jewish Congress National Archives, Montreal.)

The Jewish War Orphans Committee sent a Canadian team to Eastern Europe that included Harry Hershman and Dr. Joseph Leavitt, as Medical Director. They returned, after six months of work, bringing 146 orphans to Canada. Most of them were adopted in Montreal. Hershman himself adopted a girl.

1923 - The Federation is in deep financial trouble and a "Save the Federation Campaign" is launched, sparked by Mrs. Jacob Elkin who urges Jewish women to "wear last year's hat" to synagogue during the High Holidays, and "donate the cost of a new one to the community." Michael Hirsch chairs a general campaign that fall and the Federation has thrived ever since.

(Note—The women still wore new hats in synagogue.)

1923 - Mrs. Clarence de Sola, wife of the founding President of the Canadian Zionist Federation, is presented to the King and Queen in London. Five years earlier, she was decorated by King Albert of Belgium for assistance she organized for the Belgians during World War I.

The Wolff Girls in Girl Guide uniforms, about 1920. Direct descendants of Aaron Hart, they provided extraordinary leadership to the Montreal Jewish Community, and were recorders of history—community and family.

The Mortimer Davis Building of the YMHA is erected on Mount Royal Avenue.

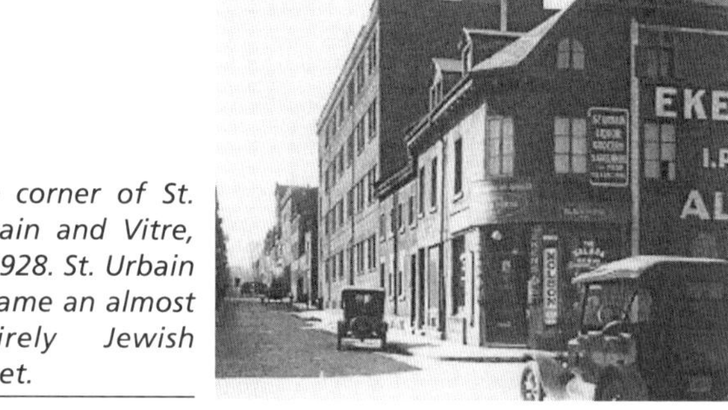

The corner of St. Urbain and Vitre, in 1928. St. Urbain became an almost entirely Jewish street.

Mark Workman — P. Abbey — Sam Bronfman — Mrs. S. Bronfman

Jack Klein — A. Mailman — J. Rost — Wal. R. Friedman

A. H. Jassby — David Kirsch — J. Levinson, Jr. — Clarence Michaels

I. Riddell — S. L. Mendelsohn — Ross Vineberg — George E. Erlick

M. Simon — J. P. Levee — H. E. Herschorn — Samuel Hart

A. Greenberg — Mrs. C. B. Fainer — Mrs. S. Jaffe — Mrs. J. Block

I. Greenberg — H. Cohen — Isidore Freedman — E. G. F. Vaz

Officers of the Jewish Federated Charities are: Honorary Campaign Chairman: Mark Workman. Campaign Chairman: Lieut.-Col. Philip Abbey. Chairmen Special Names' Committee: Zave Levinson, Clarence Michaels. Honorary Treasurer: Martin Simon. Executive Committee: Lieut.-Col. Philip Abbey, Samuel Bronfman, Isidore Freedman, Issachar Greenberg, Samuel Hart, H. E. Herschorn, A. H. Jassby, David Kirsch, J. P. Levee, J. Levinson Jr., Zave Levinson, Clarence Michaels. Executive Director: E. G. F. Vaz. Campaign Secretary: George E. Erlick. Control Committee: J. P. Levee, Convenor; Walter R. Friedman, Issachar Greenberg, Jack Klein, A. Mailman, S. L. Mendelsohn, Irving Riddell, Julius Rost, S. Ross Vineberg. Chairman Publicity Committee: Samuel Bronfman. Chairman Speakers' Committee: Horace R. Cohen. Chairman Factory Collections: A. Greenberg. Chairman Women's Division: Mrs. Samuel Bronfman. Vice-Chairman Women's Division: Mrs. C. B. [illegible] S. Jaffe. Chairmen Special Names Committee, Women's Division: Mrs. J. Block, Mrs. H. J. Levinson.

The leadership of the 1933 Federation campaign.

1931 - There are 60,087 Jews in Quebec. 94 per cent say Yiddish is their mother tongue.

Zave Ettinger told how a Chinese laundryman came to his home weekly, with a clothes hamper on wheels. He carefully identified each item—in perfect Yiddish—as he placed it in the hamper.

1931 - Allan Bronfman and Michael Hirsch co-chair a campaign despite the Great Depression to raise $800,000 to build a new "Jewish hospital." The campaign raises double its goal.

1935 - Canada admits only 880 Jewish immigrants although thousands are seeking sanctuary, as the Nazis begin their onslaught on the Jews of Germany.

1936 - Despite tales of vicious anti-Semitism in Nazi Germany, Canada admits only 619 Jews.

1937 - Only 584 Jews are admitted to Canada.

1938-1939 - As war threatened and as many as 800,000 Jews sought to flee Germany and Austria, Canada admits only 890 Jews.

1939 - Canada joins with many other countries, including the United States, in refusing to grant sanctuary to 907 Jewish refugees aboard the Saint-Louis, fleeing Nazi Germany.

A rare occurrence—a Jewish family from Germany is admitted to Canada in 1938.

Canadian villains—three of the men who denied Canada the opportunity to welcome refugees—Jews and non-Jews—fleeing Hitler's Europe.

The St. Louis, carrying refugees from Nazi Germany, is turned away by Canada, the United States and other countries. Prime Minister King, in the United States at the time, gave strict orders not to allow in any of the passengers on what became known as the "Voyage of the Damned." The German skipper, who hated the Nazis, landed his passengers in Britain and on the continent; he refused to take them back to Nazi Germany.

Warshaw's "Fruits" Market on St. Lawrence Boulevard. The owners hired a sign painter during the Depression to paint "Warsaw," on their sign—remembering their Polish roots—but when the painter made a mistake, they couldn't afford to change it.

1939-1945 - During World War II, 17,000 Canadian Jews - nearly half (8,000) from Montreal - serve in the Canadian Armed Forces.

1941 - Federation forms the Combined Jewish Appeal in collaboration with the Jewish General Hospital, and the United Jewish Refugee and War Relief Agencies.

1942 - The Jewish Hospital of Hope for the chronically ill is created in east-end Montreal. It was first, ill-advisedly, called the "Incurable Hospital!"

1944 - Jewish Vocational Service becomes a functioning agency. The idea had first been approved by Federation in 1938 (to be called the Jewish Vocational Guidance Bureau), but the outbreak of World War II delayed creation of the agency.

1944 - The Hillel Foundation is created to serve Jewish University students. When the war ends, thousands of Jewish servicemen flock to universities.

1947-1952 - 11,064 Jews are admitted to Canada. 40 per cent of them choose to settle in Montreal. Canadian Jewish Congress negotiates a deal whereby 2,136 tailors and 500 furriers—60 per cent Jewish—are admitted. While Quebec nationalists opposed the entry of European Jews, in Montreal alone, refugees founded 31 new industrial plants in a single year.

1947 - 1,100 youngsters—some survivors of concentration camps, some emerging from hiding places, are welcomed to Canada. 525 settle in Montreal. Months later, Congress had to seek permission, which was granted, for the parents of some of the "orphans" to be admitted.

Squadron Leader Sydney Shulemson, DSO, DFC, of Montreal—Canada's most decorated Jewish World War II warrior. Leading formations of Beaufort fighter-bombers, he destroyed and sank a number of German vessels. (Canadian Jewish Congress National Archives, Montreal)

The Federation building.

1949 - Federation moves into its own building at 493 Sherbrooke West, near McGill University.

1950 - Prime Minister Louis St. Laurent appoints Harry Batshaw to the Quebec Superior Court. He is the first Jew named to the bench in Canada. Mr. Batshaw was the son of an immigrant carpenter.

1950 - The National Council of Jewish Women starts work on forming what became the Golden Age Association. Florence Kirshner was the first, part-time director, for an agency located in a house. It was to grow into one of the most outstanding agencies, anywhere, serving seniors.

1951 - The Ezra Ladies Group receives a charter to operate a convalescent home. It became, in time, the modern Jewish Rehabilitation Hospital.

1952 - The Jewish population of Montreal reaches 85,000. (The census shows there are 34 Jews living in Cote St. Luc.)

1956 - The outbreak of the Hungarian Revolution triggers another wave of refugees and, of 4,500 Hungarian Jews, more than 1,500 choose to live in Montreal.

David Katz conducting the Golden Age Association's Naginah Orchestra.

1957-1966 - more than 3,000 Moroccan Jews, fleeing anti-Semitism in the North African Kingdom, emigrate to Canada and three-quarters choose Montreal as their new home.

1959 - A capital fund campaign raises $2,800,000 which—with a $1,100,000 Federal-Provincial Grant—paves the way for construction of a new Hospital and Home for the Aged—ultimately called the Maimonides Geriatric Centre. It was opened in 1965.

Jewish immigrants greeted in Montreal in the 1950s at JIAS headquarters on Esplanade Avenue.

Eleanor London, founding Chief Librarian of the Public Library now bearing her name.

1963 - The Baron de Hirsch Institute celebrates its centenary, and Executive Director David Weiss writes: "The Institute is a living expression of the ageless Jewish precepts of mitzvah (good deeds) and tzedakah (social justice), of Jeremiah's injunction to seek the welfare of the city in which one's own welfare is achieved."

1966 - The (largely-Jewish) City of Cote St. Luc establishes a public library, hiring Eleanor London to develop the facility.

The Library, acknowledged as the best public library in Greater Montreal, began on an upper floor of the old City Hall ("I had a rickety desk and some pencils"), moved to the Cote St. Luc Shopping Centre and then to its own premises on Cavendish Boulevard. Ultimately, the Library is named in honour of its founding Chief Librarian, who served for three and a half decades.

1967 - The Saidye Bronfman Centre of the YMHA is opened—a gift, from her four children, to honour Mrs. Samuel Bronfman, O.B.E., on her birthday.

1967 - With Arab nations threatening to "drive the Jews into the Sea", Samuel Bronfman summoned Jewish leaders from coast to coast, to an emergency meeting at the Montefiore Club.

Mr. Sam tripled his gift to the Combined Jewish Appeal and called on the others to follow suit. Most of them did.

The Judaism Pavilion at Expo '67, the Montreal World's Fair

The idea for the meeting came up in the Bronfman's private jet as Community leaders were en route to a State dinner in Quebec City for the President of Israel. The gloomy discussion, prior to the decision, involved Federation President Jacob Loewy and Executive Committee Chairman Gordon Brown.

The trio, scanning newspaper reports, felt Israel could be destroyed. In fact, a few days later, Israeli forces thundered to an incredible six day victory over the combined armies of its Arab enemies.

1969 - The nurses' residence of the Jewish Hospital of Hope is converted to become the Jewish Nursing Home.

1970 - Victor Charles Goldbloom becomes the first member of the Jewish Community to become a Quebec cabinet minister.

Premier Robert Bourassa named Dr. Goldbloom Minister of State Responsible for Quality of Environment; three years later, he became Minister of Municipal Affairs, resigning in 1979 when Claude Ryan became party leader.

Habitat '67, the innovative 158-unit architectural development designed by Israeli-born Moshe Safdie. The apartment complex was built by assembling prefabricated concrete blocks and has been described as "an indisputable architectural and engineering tour de force."

1971 - Samuel Bronfman House is opened on Dr. Wilder Penfield Avenue as the National Headquarters of Canadian Jewish Congress. After Congress moves to Cummings House, the building is taken over by the Jewish Studies Program of Concordia University, but the immense Congress Archives remain in a lower level of the building.

1971 - Federation, the Jewish General Hospital and other agencies team up to create the Montreal Jewish Community Foundation, with Arthur Pascal as its first President and Harry Berger the first executive director.

The Montreal Expos baseball team is founded under the leadership of Charles Rosner Bronfman. Attending the opening game is Samuel Bronfman, Charles' father (centre) with Prime Minister Lester Bowles Pearson on his left and Governor General Roland Michener on his right.

1972 - Following the westward flow of the Jewish Community, Federation moves into its new home—Cummings House.

Born in Saint John, NB, in 1898, Maxwell Cummings lived to be 103, experiencing three different centuries. Mr. Cummings, and his older brother Nathan, had gone into business in 1911 in Montreal. Nathan moved to the United States, where he rose to great prominence in the business and art worlds. Maxwell went into real estate brokerage and development, beginning in 1929.

Gordon Brown who served as President of Federation 1967-1969, had been General Chairman of the Combined Jewish Appeal in 1961. On assuming the Presidency, he left his business affairs to his partners and moved into the Federation building. Working with close associates, including Joe Ain and Boris G. Levine, he provided a remarkable dimension of leadership to the community.

Morley M. Cohen was General Chairman of the 1969 Combined Jewish Appeal, chaired a capital funds campaign for the YM-YWHA and was President, for more than a decade, of Canadian Friends of Haifa University.

The Cummings name adorns Federation's headquarters and a seniors' recreational facility.

1972 - The community is stunned by the figures in a Federally-funded Study showing that one Jewish Montrealer in six (about 20,000 people) live at or below the poverty line.

1973 - The March to Jerusalem is created and draws about 20,000 participants annually—making it the biggest such event in North America. Jewish communities worldwide press the Jewish Cultural Association, headed by Manny Spinner, for details of how the March is organized and a handbook for wide distribution is prepared.

1975 - The Jewish Education Council is formed to strengthen the system. Charles Bronfman sold the educators on the concept of a coordinating body.

1976 - The nationalist Parti Québécois, led by René Lévesque, is elected, and thousands of Quebecers, concerned about the future of the province under a separatist government, move out. The Jewish population of Montreal begins a steady decline, and the Toronto Jewish community quickly becomes the largest in Canada. Within five years of the election, 20,000 Jews had left Montreal.

1976 - Author Saul Bellow becomes the first Montrealer to win a Nobel Prize.

1977 - Federation begins support for Project Genesis, a storefront operation to assist the poor, Jewish and otherwise, in the Cote des Neiges area. Later, the Project opens branches in Jerusalem and Amman, Jordan. The key figure in organizing the project was McGill Professor Jim Torczyner.

1978 - The Nathan and Maxwell Cummings Golden Age Centre is opened. It is one of the most modern facilities of its kind in Canada. Both Cummings (Nathan and Maxwell) brothers attended the dedication of the building.

Author Mordecai Richler receives, in 1969, (for Cocksure*) his first Governor General's Award. His second came in 1972 (for* St. Urbain's Horseman*). He is seen here with filmmaker Alan Handel and cinematographer Barry Perles as they prepare for the theatrical debut of Richler's* The Apprenticeship of Duddy Kravitz *at the Saidye Bronfman Centre.*

On Richler's death, in 2001, Prime Minister Jean Chretien paid tribute to the author, declaring "he was simply one of the most brilliant, original and celebrated artists in Canadian history."

Boris G. Levine, FCA, President of Federation 1969-1971, became the first and only former President to assume the onerous task of also serving as General Chairman of the Combined Jewish Appeal.

The March to Jerusalem in Montreal.

Maxwell Cummings (seated), who with his brother Nathan was the principal funder of the new Cummings House, tours the new building. With him, (l. to r.) Danyael Cantor, Executive Vice-President; President Marilyn Blumer; Norma (Mrs. Jack) Cummings; grandson Steven Cummings; granddaughter Nancy Cummings Gold, and her husband, Marc Gold.

Jewish Community leaders meet with the first Parti Québécois Premier, René Lévesque (right). Participating in the meeting are (clockwise from top left) Ralph Lallouz, Harvey Crestohl, Manuel Weiner, Joel Pinsky and Alan Rose. (Canadian Jewish Congress National Archives, Montreal)

Samuel Bronfman (right, at podium) is honoured at his 80th birthday party with the presentation of the first Bronfman Medal—Canadian Jewry's highest communal award. The presentor is Munroe Abbey.

Sheila Kussner (second from l.) is presented with the Samuel Bronfman Medal, the community's highest honour. With her (l. to r.) are Marilyn Blumer, President of Federation; Dodo Heppner, Chair of the Bronfman Medal Committee; and Freda Rashkoven, Chair of the Federation's Awards Committee.

1979 - Canada's first Holocaust Museum is opened in Cummings House.

1981 - The Auxiliary of the Sir Mortimer B. Davis Jewish General Hospital initiates "Hope and Cope," an imaginative support program for cancer patients and their families. The concept, which has been hailed by many other institutions internationally, was the result of the leadership of Sheila Kussner.

1983 - Alan B. Gold is appointed Chief Justice of the Superior Court of Quebec.

1984 - The Jewish Public Library highlighted its 70th Anniversary by officially opening its Archives Department.

1985 - The Convalescent Hospital changes its name to the Jewish Rehabilitation Hospital, reflecting its enhanced treatment programs.

1985 - Herbert Marx is named Quebec Justice Minister; he resigns in 1988 and, in 1994, he is appointed a Justice of the Superior Court.

1986 - Mount Sinai Hospital, located for decades in the Laurentians, is moved to Cote St. Luc and, in addition to treating respiratory diseases, undertakes chronic care. And the Jewish Nursing Home moves to land west of the Jewish General Hospital and expands from 44 to 160 beds.

1988 - Montreal students participate in the first March of the Living, experiencing the emotional reality of the Holocaust, in Poland and then wind up their visit in Israel.

Chief Justice Alan B. Gold

1989 - Auberge Shalom, a shelter for women victims of conjugal violence and their children, is established by the National Council of Jewish Women.

The Council made its move after a Jewish woman in a Montreal suburb, Donna Kertzer Rose, was murdered in 1984.

1989 - Sidney Altman, son of a Montreal grocer, wins a Nobel Prize in Chemistry.

1992 - Rudolph Marcus becomes the third Montrealer to win a Nobel Prize and the second to win the award in chemistry.

1994 - Sylviane Borenstein is the first Jewish woman appointed to the Quebec Bench, when she is named to the Superior Court.

1996 - A survey by Federation/CJA indicates that more than one quarter of Montreal Jews expect to leave Quebec in the next five years. "All the problems experienced here by the Jewish community are connected to the secession issue and political uncertainty," noted Jack Jedwab, Director of the Quebec Region of Canadian Jewish Congress.

Charles Shahar, author of the study, stated "the community has reached an historic crossroads, where important choices have to be made in order to ensure not just the survival of the Jewish presence in Montreal, but to make sure that it continues to be a vibrant cultural and religious centre."

Mr. Justice Herbert Marx.

Phyllis Lambert, in 1989, created the Canadian Centre for Architecture in Montreal. It is one of the greatest institutions in the world in the field of architecture.

Two Governor General's Award winners—author Naim Kattan and artist Ghitta Caiserman-Roth.

Norman Spector is named Canadian Ambassador to Israel, serving until 1995.

Morton Brownstein (left) is presented with the Jewish General Hospital Distinguished Service Award by Leo Goldfarb, Chair of the Awards.

Thomas Hecht with Quebec Premier Lucien Bouchard.

1997 - Thomas O. Hecht becomes the first Jew and the second anglophone appointed to the Board of Directors of the Caisse de dépôt et placement du Québec.

Born in Czechoslovakia, in 1929, Thomas Hecht and his family managed to thread their way through chaotic wartime Europe to Lisbon, Portugal, where they boarded an overloaded vessel for the Atlantic crossing.

They made their way to Montreal, from New York, at the very end of 1941.

Mr. Hecht became the youngest Chairman ever of the Combined Jewish Appeal in 1970, and in the '80s he served, for five years, as President of the Israel Bond Organization. He was also President of the Canada-Israel Committee for 15 years.

1999 - Sheila Finestone, Liberal Member of Parliament for Mount Royal from 1984, is named to the Senate. Mrs. Finestone played a number of leadership roles in the activities of the Jewish Community.

Rosalind Goodman, with Yoine Goldstein, is presented with the Distinguished Leadership Award of Federation/CJA in 1997.

1999 - The new Jewish Community Campus is inaugurated at Number One Cummings Square.

2000 - The Hospital of Hope and the Jewish Nursing Home merge to form the Jewish Eldercare Centre.

The Montreal Jewish Community Foundation is listed as the fifth largest body of its kind in Canada. Leaders of the Foundation pictured here include (l. to r.) Robert Kleinman, Executive Vice-President; Robert Vineberg, Senior Vice-President; Marilyn Blumer, President of Federation/CJA; Milly Lande, the Foundation's "Woman of the Year"; Foundation President Stanley Hyman and Executive-Director Joel King. By 2004, the Foundation boasted $160,000,000 in assets.

Hon. Sheila Finestone

The Twenty-First Century

2001 - The census estimates 80,390 Jews live in Montreal (a loss of about 11 per cent in five years).

2002 - Federation/CJA president Steven Cummings told his organization's 85th Annual General Meeting that "Montreal is experiencing an upsurge in Jewish immigration." He added, "In the last three months, requests concerning immigration to Montreal have tripled from distressed communities."

2002 - David Levine becomes the first Jewish cabinet minister in a Parti Québécois government. He became the third Jewish Cabinet minister in Quebec history— following Victor Goldbloom and Herbert Marx.

Ben Weider (right) at the dedication of the newly-named Ben Weider Jewish Community Centre, in 2001. The Centre was renamed after Mr. Weider, the major donor, underwrote a $15,000,000 facelift for the Snowdon YM-YWHA. Others in the photo (l. to r.) are Rabbi Sidney Shoham, Gary Shapiro, Chairman of the Building Committee; and President Doreen Green.

Lawrence Bergman was named Quebec Revenue Minister in 2003. Mr. Bergman was first elected to the National Assembly in 1994 and was re-elected in 1998 and 2003.

2003 - Morris Fish of Montreal becomes the second Jew named to the Supreme Court of Canada.

2003 - A unique study of the *frum* (Orthodox) community by Montreal's Federation/CJA showed there are 11,025 *frum* individuals in Montreal—or about 12 per cent of the city's Jewish population of 92,970. Almost half were under 15 years of age compared with less than 20 per cent for the broader Jewish community.

2004 - A Federation study of Jewish poverty showed that 18.4 per cent of the Jewish population—-17,110—were living below the poverty line.

The study suggested that the proportion of poor Jews is rising.

It was 15.4 per cent in 1971, and has risen every year according to the census. 3,225 are "working poor." That is, they have jobs but they don't earn enough to rise above the poverty line.

Those particularly affected are the elderly, single parent females and a large number of children.

2005 - Montreal lawyer Yoine Goldstein is named to the Canadian Senate. An internationally-prominent attorney, Mr. Goldstein also has devoted an extraordinary amount of time to community affairs.

Member of Parliament Irwin Cotler was named Canada's Minister of Justice and Attorney General of Canada in 2003, after a four-year stint as a Member of Parliament.

Montreal's Nobel Laureates

The official population of the city of Montreal is 3,326,510. Of this number, about 80,000 are Jews—that is, about 2 ½ per cent. Three Montrealers have won Nobel Prizes—Saul Bellow in Literature (1976) and two chemists—Sidney Altman and Rudolph Marcus (1989 and 1992). All three Nobel Laureates are Jewish!

Part Two

PERSONALITY PROFILES

David J. Azrieli, C.M., C.Q.

DAVID J. AZRIELI, C.M., C.Q., B.A,.M. ARCH, MRAIC, ASSOC. AIA

(Honorary Degrees: LL.D., D.H.L., D. Sc., Ph.D., D. Arch.)

David J. Azrieli was appointed to the Order of Canada in 1984.

Prior to this, in 1983, Yeshiva University in New York conferred on him an Honorary Doctorate in Humane Letters (D.H.L.). In 1975, Concordia University had conferred on him a Doctor of Laws degree.

Since the appointment, he has been honoured by the following institutions:

In 1985, Technion University, his Alma Mater, conferred on him an Honorary Doctorate of Science in Technology (D. Sc.).

In 1996, Tel Aviv University in Israel conferred on him an Honorary Doctorate of Philosophy.

In 1998, Mr. Azrieli received the Israeli Prime Minister's Jubilee Award for his contributions to the Israeli economy.

In 1999, he was named Chevalier to the Ordre national du Québec.

In 2001, he made a gift to the Montreal Museum of Fine Arts, of an 1895 oil by Renoir.

In 2001, he was named Honorary Fellow of the City of Jerusalem.

In 2002, he was named Honorary Fellow of the Board of Governors of Shenkar College of Engineering and Design.

In 2003, he received a doctorate degree in Architecture, Honoris Causa, from Carleton University, Ottawa.

Over the years, Mr. Azrieli has been actively involved in pursuing his love of architecture and education and has been instrumental in promoting and supporting studies in architecture at various levels in different countries. Other accomplishments include:

- Chair in Architecture and Town Planning, Technion Institute of Technology
- Chair in Urban and Environmental Architecture, Tel Aviv University
- The Azrieli School of Architecture, Tel Aviv University, 1994
- The Azrieli Graduate School of Jewish Education and Administration, Yeshiva University, N.Y., 1983

- Established the First Graduate Scholarship at Concordia University, 1975
- Established the Azrieli Holocaust Library Collection, Concordia University, 1982
- In 1995, he completed his studies and earned a Master of Architecture degree with distinction from Carleton University.
- In 2000, he established the David J. Azrieli Institute for Graduate Studies in Architecture at Carleton University.
- He also established the Azrieli Integrated Centre for the Advancement of Youth—a project to prevent teens from dropping out of school.
- In 2002, he established the Azrieli Foundation Graduate Fellowship in Holocaust Studies at Concordia University.

Mr. Azrieli is:

- Member and past Vice-Chairman, International Board of Governors, Technion, Israel Institute of Technology, and a board member
- Member of the Board of Governors, Tel Aviv University
- Member of the Board of Trustees, Bezalel Academy of Art and Design, Jerusalem
- Member of the Board of Trustees, Yeshiva University, New York
- Past National President and Honorary President of the Canadian Zionist Federation
- Past National President and Honorary President, Canadian Technion Society
- Chairman of the Advisory and Member of the Board of the Canada-Israel Chamber of Commerce

In addition to his daily involvement in business operations, Mr. Azrieli spends time every day working for the good of the community. His efforts are dedicated to education and philanthropy.

The Greatest Bagels and Briskets

There is no question that Montreal bagels and briskets are among the best, if not the best in the world. And it was a Russian Jewish immigrant who introduced the bagel to Montrealers. But, when you delve into the knotty question of who first provided Montreal with smoked meat, you run into considerable controversy.

The same apparently is not true about bagels. There appears to be general agreement that a Russian immigrant, Chaim Seligman (born in 1880, in Russia as Zelikman) introduced the bagel to Montreal in 1900, with his Montreal Bagel Bakery.

There are differences between New York and Toronto bagels, on the one hand, and the Montreal product, on the other. In Montreal, the ovens are heated with wood. In other cities, bakers are forced, by law, to use gas-fired ovens.

Montreal's bagel pioneer—Chaim Seligman, at his granddaughter's wedding.

You never hear of anyone demanding, for example, that someone bring back bagels from a visit to Toronto. In fact, *Fodor's Guidebook* calls Montreal "Canada's Bagel Capital". Seligman strung his bagels into dozens, and from his St. Lawrence Boulevard oven, patrolled the streets of the Jewish Main, (graduating from, in time, a pushcart to a horse and wagon, and then to a fliver; his granddaughter Miriam recalls that when she was about 6, she would accompany him as he delivered bagels from the rear, or rumble seat, of what apparently had been a taxi).

Two of his employees were once partners, but they had a falling out and created St. Viateur Bagel and Fairmount Bagel.

The Russian-born baker had first worked in Lachine, providing the sizeable Jewish community there with European-style bread early in the century (he came to Canada in 1902), and then began baking bagels in an oven located in a lane next door to what is now Schwartz's Deli.

Legend has it that the bagel was originated in Vienna, in 1683, by a Jewish baker. He wanted to thank the King of Poland for saving the Austrian capital from attacking Turks. The baker created a small bread in the form of a stirrup. The Austrian word for stirrup is "beugel."

Fans of St. Viateur Bagel, run by Meyer Lewkowitz, included Prince Charles. One Saturday, when the line outside the shop coiled around to Park Avenue, the telephone rang and a cultured voice announced, "I'd like to order 20 dozen bagels for Prince Charles." The harried chap answering the call angrily responded, "Stop kidding around. We're busy here." And he hung up. An hour later, three handsome black limousines pulled up outside the bagel shop and a naval officer, readily identifiable as escort to someone of great importance, emerged from the lead vehicle and, disregarding the long line-up, marched up to the counter and declared, haughtily, "I'm here for Prince Charles' bagels." The Prince was in town with a Royal Navy

Squadron and presumably he was in one of the limousines. The clerk didn't miss a beat. "You'll have to get in line like everyone else." Not arguing, the naval officer obediently got into line, waited for close to an hour before he was able to pick up "Prince Charles' bagels" and disappeared once more into the lead limousine.

Apparently, smoked meat was brought to Montreal by Ben Kravitz, a Lithuanian immigrant who reached Canada in 1899, aged 17, with limited assets ($15 and a bullet wound in his heel!). His wife, Fanny, set up a sandwich shop in 1908, for factory workers—offering fruit, cookies and ordinary sandwiches. When the hungry girls asked for something more substantial, Ben remembered how his grandparents prepared smoked meat.

Their first café was on St. Lawrence Boulevard, at Duluth; in 1929, they moved downtown to the northwest corner of Metcalfe Street and de Maisonneuve Boulevard. Finally, they crossed the road, in 1950, to the southeast corner where they have stayed for more than half a century.

All purveyors of smoked meat claim that they have the best recipe for preparing briskets, but not one of them is willing to divulge their secrets. It is known, however, that Kravitz chose very lean briskets, smothered them with salt, garlic, herbs and spices before smoking them for days. In the the final stage, the briskets were steamed for several hours.

The first sandwiches cost 5 cents and were not, in the beginning, popular. (A whole meal dished out by Fanny Kravitz cost 20 cents, early in the century.)

During the Great Depression, Kravitz would personally provide food to those who lined up outside his restaurant. This was Ben's "bread-line."

That, of course, changed and by 1939, the Main featured European-style delis, cheek-by-jowl, offering various types of smoked meat (as distinct from pastrami, from the Turkish "bedim"—and

Schwartz's Deli, on the Main, in 1927 and 80 years later.

corned beef). In one block there were seven delicatessens, a smoked meat Mecca, so to speak. But the price had soared to 10 cents.

Delis such as Etinson's, Putter's, Shagass', Rogatko and Chenoy competed for the sandwich trade, each with their own version of smoked meat. And each had a substantial following. But Maurice and Reuben Schwartz appear to have snatched the gold ring when, in 1927, they opened their deli, featuring Romanian smoked meat. Schwartz's, with a variety of owners, has dominated the scene on the Main, ever since—the last survivor of the golden era. The original smoker, installed by Reuben in 1930, at latest word was still being used.

During the years after the Second World War, Ezekiel Bronfman, visiting Montreal, would bring his grandsons, Edward and Charles, to Ben's where the boys would tuck into smoked meat sandwiches, while Grandpa spoke to Kravitz—in Yiddish, of course.

The Jewish ghetto called the Main, which existed for about half a century in downtown Montreal, was a third solitude—totally different from its French neighbours (to the east) and the English (to the west). One of the major differences was language. On the Main, Yiddish was widely used.

Distinctive foods helped bridge the gap.

Once a few people sampled bagels and briskets, customers flocked to lower St. Lawrence Boulevard. Today, those in charge of promoting Montreal tourism mainly plug French cuisine, but they make room for bagels and briskets, too.

One woman recalls how her mother sent her to the deli for "scraps," which cost 5 cents. The girl thought that "scraps" was a cut of meat, not the leftovers. But the mother stretched the tiny bits of smoked meat into a meal for herself, her husband and her brood.

The Smoked Meat Mile in Montreal circa 1939 on St. Lawrence Blvd. (the Main):

4442 - Rogatko's	**4563 - Putter's**
4304 - Montreal Labour Committee for Palestine	**4447 - Chenoy's Brooklyn**
4226 - JIAS office	4379 - Finkel's Herring Store
4094 - Abie's Sanitary Barbershop	4169 - Labow's Cut-Rate Drugstore
3828 - St. Lawrence Bakery	4101 - Hebrew National
3750 - Shap's Lunch	4075 - Eagle Publishing
	4067-4069 - Horn's Restaurant
	3895 - Schwartz's
	3877 - Montreal Hebrew
	3859 - Warsaw Bargain Fruit Market

Note - the Delis are marked in bold letters.
The one survivor is Schwartz's, which opened in 1927.

Horn's Restaurant

Will Be Open During the
Passover Holidays --- and
Serve Passover Meals

FOR YOUR HEALTH — EAT AT

Horn's

4069 ST. LAWRENCE BLVD.

By 2002, barely half a dozen of the old Jewish firms were still doing business on the Main. One of the closures that year was the landmark Warshaw's Supermarket. A careless sign-maker had added the "h" to Warsaw, after which the owners had named their estalishment 67 years earlier. It had been too expensive, at the time, to change it and so it remained.

In October, 2002, the Federal Government recognized the Main as an historic site for "its role as a home and workplace for generations of Jewish immigrants."

Toronto-born artist Sidney Berne's painting of Schwartz's deli on the Main. Berne (real name Bernstein) is popular for his paintings of Montreal memories—particularly St. Viateur Bagel, the deli and the Bagg Street Synagogue.

Baron Byng High School (1921-1980)

In 1921, the Protestant School Board of Greater Montreal (PSBGM) built a high school on St. Urbain Street and named it, grandiosely, in honour of Governor-General Lord Byng of Vimy, who opened the school, himself, in 1922.

Mordecai Richler was one of the best-known Baron Byng students

The PSBGM had set out to ghettoize Jewish students, funnelling them largely into this institution.

Historian/archivist David Rome wrote, "It was built by the Protestant authorities to segregate the growing number of Jewish high school students from the Christians, and to help keep the High School of Montreal more nearly 'clean of Jews.' "

But, whatever they planned, it backfired. The school graduated some of the most important figures in Montreal history.

The Gazette reported, in a 1980 story, "for decades, Baron Byng students led the province in the high school leaving exams."

Richler wrote about the school:

"We were the progeny of taxi drivers, clothing factory cutters, junk dealers, peddlers and sewing machine operators, enjoined to do better or else, and so we did."

Sid Stevens, a proud graduate of Baron Byng, now utilizes the building for his Sun Youth organization. He recalls, "Mordecai Richler went here; David Lewis went here; Harry Blank went here; Dr. Phil Gold, the famous surgeon on cancer, went here; many other famous people. This was THE school because this was a Jewish Ghetto between 1940 and 1965."

Baron Byng grad Morris Fish was named to the Supreme Court of Canada.

—Outstanding Graduates—

Baron Byng graduates included:

Supreme Court Justice Morris Fish (he was known as "Big Moe" and, in the year book, he said his ambition was to be a criminal lawyer) ; Mr. Justice Herbert Marx, one-time provincial cabinet minister; Superior Court Judge Nathan Tannenbaum; Mr. Justice Louis S. Tannenbaum of the Quebec Superior Court; actor William Shatner (*Star Trek*, etc.) and actress Marilyn Lightstone (*Lies My Father Told Me*), and that film's producer, Harry Gulkin; Stephen Pinker, a major figure in modern psychology, and author of books on how the mind works; Nobel Prize winner Rudolph Markus (chemistry) ; Concordia University Rector Dr. Frederick Lowy; one-time Federal Cabinet Minister Gerry Weiner; *Gazette* columnist Mike Boone; war correspondent Lionel Shapiro (who wanted to be a dental technician); and communications specialist Stanley Asher.

Other important graduates included:

Much-decorated World War II pilot Sydney Shulemson; novelist Mordecai Richler; banker James D. Raymond; businesman/publisher Amos Sochaczevski.

David Lewis, a Baron Bynger, says he met the two "most important people in (his) life" at Baron Byng—his wife, Sophie, and poet A.M. Klein.

William Shatner of Star Trek *fame attended Baron Byng.*

Still more Baron Byng alumni:

Rhodes scholar David Lewis, who became head of the New Democratic Party; cancer specialist Dr. Phil Gold; endocrinologist Dr. Allen Gold; two of Montreal's top surgeons, Harvey Sigman and Nathan Sheiner; neurosurgeon Harold Jacob Rosen; Dr. Joseph Portnoy; Dr. Leonard Pinsky, head of McGill University's Department of Human Genetics;
accountant Abbey Kreisman (who said, on graduation, his ambition was to be a mining engineer!);
poets Irving Layton (who was expelled) and A.M. Klein;
Member of Parliament Fred Rose (who was arrested as a Soviet spy);
sociologist Lionel Tiger;
labour lawyer Laddie Schnaiberg;
National Assembly member Harry Blank (who remembered that hot dogs were "two for a nickel up the street") ;
Mel Dobrin, who headed up the Steinberg grocery empire, and flew 32 missions in the Royal Canadian Air Force in World War II;
Michael Fainstat, one-time Chair of the Montreal Executive Committee;
one-time Cote St. Luc Mayor Bernard Lang;
journalist and historian Abe Arnold; the head of B'nai Brith, Bill Surkis;
Seymour Schulich, Chairman and CEO of Franco-Nevada Corporation, and Ned Goodman, CEO of the financial sevices firm Dundee Wealth Management Inc.;
Professor Adam Fuerstenberg, an authority on Yiddish literature;
Bertram Greenford who built Bronfman House;
Senator Yoine Goldstein, an outstanding lawyer and community leader.

Other distinguished grads included:

The class of 1926 included poet A.M. Klein.

artists Moe Reinblatt, Seymour Segal and Sylvia Ary; Aaron Fish, who invented the pushbutton lock, and who wrote, "In June 1949, I put my trombone down and began peddling keys. Starting with my initial capital of $20, a bike and $100 of borrowed keys, I built up a company which today employs 3,700 people world-wide with sales of $500-million. We still make only locks and keys.";

Jack Rabinovitch, Richler's buddy, who established the annual $25,000 Giller literary prize (to honour his wife).

Not everybody was a good citizen. Graduates included Harry Ship, a racketeer. Some students did things differently. Norman Spector, later head of a major heating oil company, and head of both the Combined Jewish Appeal and Israel Bonds, was known as "the kid who never goes to school". Norm juggled classes with three part-time jobs!

Baron Byng Class of 1926.

Baron Byng Class of 1931.

One unsung hero (or heroine) was Natalie Rosenfeld-Bercovici who devoted much of her life to helping Montrealers overcome poverty, hunger and despair—first through her volunteer work at the Old Brewery Mission, 1993-1998, and then as a founder of Generations Foundation, providing meals for more than 4,800 needy school children daily.

Not everybody made it. Lillian Rabinovitch Reinblatt had to drop out; she couldn't afford the monthly fees. Later, as a lawyer, she became a television personality on CFCF-TV's *People in Conflict*.

Syd Ross remembers that, as an Air Cadet, he was supposed to wear black shoes with his uniform, but "we were too poor," so he shamefacedly wore his regular brown oxfords.

School fees were a problem. Eddie Champagne and Sam Levy (class of 1939) wrote:

"Going to high school was not free in 1935. The monthly fee of $2 in Grade 8, rose to $5 in Grade 11, and $10 in Grade 12—major sums in those days for low-income families with several children attending school. The dropout rate of 25 per cent during the four years was due as much to financial causes as to scholastic ones."

Champagne and Levy noted further that "although 98 per cent of the student body at Baron Byng was Jewish, we counted only three Jewish teachers on staff due to the policies of the Protestant School Board of Greater Montreal."

Rudolph A. Marcus, winner of the Nobel Prize in Chemistry in 1992, stated, "My education at Baron Byng High School was excellent, with dedicated masters."

Some outstanding educators included Dr. J.S. Astbury, the principal, who insisted on the highest standards from teacher and pupil alike, English teacher Mr. Saunders whose reading of a poem with such eloquence and passion inspired student Irving Layton to become a poet, the Welsh choirmaster D.M. Herbert, who introduced the students to fine music, particularly choir singing (after all, he was Welsh), and art teacher Anne Savage, who inspired a whole generation of art students.

Rudolph A. Marcus

Richler's "Fletcher's Field High" alias Baron Byng High School:

Mordecai Richler would refer to Baron Byng High in his novels, but labelled it "Fletcher's Field High". The author wrote about the school in The Street, *noting: "The school became something of a legend in our area. Everybody, it seemed, had passed though FFHS. Canada's most famous gambler, an Atom Bomb spy. Boys who went off to fight in the Spanish Civil War. Miracle-making doctors and silver-tongued lawyers. Boxers. Fighters for Israel. Again and again we led Quebec province in the Junior matriculation results."*

Baron Byng High was built on St. Urbain Street, in the heart of the Jewish Community, in 1921.

Despite the fact that Jews made up a tiny fraction of the population of Montreal, the strong emphasis on education saw the number of Jewish students, in 1922, exceed Christians in Protestant schools—1,534 to 1,305.

Baron Byng was more than 90 per cent Jewish. The Class of 1939, including accountant Edward Wolkove, boasted it was "100 per cent Jewish." Wolkove delivered for a drugstore to help pay the $3.50 Grade 9 monthly high school fee.

Montreal journalist Charles Lazarus (Class of '35) wrote in the *Montreal Star* that Baron Byng High would go down in history as a "most unusual high school which, through the years, has produced its own aristocracy in the arts, sciences, letters, politics, sports, education, and the law—both the enforcement of and aversion to."

Facing Anti-Semitism

When they emerged from high school, they would face the problem of quotas in universities.

McGill University would accept only seven Jews in its medical program. And Jewish kids had to run up marks better by 10 per cent to even be considered.

Twins Bernard and Sidney Lerman ran into this barrier. Bernard came first in the province and his brother came second, but McGill wouldn't take two from the same family. So Sidney went to McGill, and Bernard went to an American university.

World War II

World War II changed everything, of course. About 90 per cent of the boys in the class of 1939 enlisted. The first to die was Joe Gertel who was fatally wounded on D-Day, June 6, 1944. In all, 35 "Byngers" died in the conflict.

Sidney Phillips escaped from an Italian prisoner of war camp and made it back to the Allies' lines.

Some students, for a lark, climbed onto the school roof and painted a bull's-eye thereon—suggesting it would make a great target should the Luftwaffe venture that far afield.

Some others from the class of '39 included Isaac Welt, computer science professor at the American University in Washington; Dr. Gilbert Rosenberg, Medical Director of the St. Mary of the Lakes Geriatric Centre in Kingston, Ontario; McGill mathematics professor Sam Melamed; Dr. Sam Levy, chief biochemist of The Queen Elizabeth Hospital; Rubin Shucher, chief chemist at the Jewish General Hospital; and pharmacist Cecil Labow.

Among those in the class of '44 was Harry Gonschar who was smart enough to become a student with Albert Einstein. Among those in the class of '49 were Nicolas Steinmetz, planning director for the McGill University Health Centre, and Zipporah Dunsky-Shnay, director of the Jewish Public Library.

The Class of '52 boasted about its doctors, including Harry Bard, head of Gerontology at Ste. Justine Hospital; cardiologist Ernie Fallen; dermatologist Aaron Glick; radiologist Marvin Nathans; Leonard Pinsky, who chaired the Human Genetics Department at McGill University; Arthur Rosenberg, head of Haematology at the Jewish General Hospital; Maynard Shapiro, head of Plastic Surgery at the JGH; and Jack Mendelson, who was Chief of Infectious Diseases at the JGH.

As well, Joan (Cantor) Shuter was a clinical psychologist, and Herman Gelber was a psychiatrist.

Moshe Pripstein became senior physicist at the University of California at Berkeley.

Baron Byng High School closed in 1980. By that time, most of its students were Greek.

Ben Greenberg and the Kiki Gang

Being a Jewish policeman in Montreal during the1920s and 1930s wasn't easy. Many who joined the force dropped out because of vicious anti-Semitism. One who didn't was Ben Greenberg, a burly 250 pounder who could hold his own quite handily. In fact, Ben rose to be a detective inspector, in the northern portion of the Main. One of his major concerns was the Kiki Gang, which harassed and robbed people in the area. Ben received a tip one day that the gang was holed up in a tenement and, gathering a number of uniformed cops, he raided the building. Sure enough, the gang was all assembled on the ground floor, and Ben and his coppers collared the lot—all but the leader. "Where's your boss?" Ben demanded of one gang member, raising him off the ground with one powerful hand. "He's upstairs, asleep," the gang member admitted. Greenberg pounded up the stairs—two at a time—and flung open the bedroom door. And, sure enough, the Kiki kingpin was in bed—but he was not asleep. Instead, he brandished a pistol—and it was aimed at Ben's ample chest. "I just reacted without thinking," Ben explained later. He leaped, recklessly, onto the thug in the bed. The revolver went off—missing Ben. And the combined weight of the two muscular men was too much for the bed. It collapsed—and the floor of the rickety tenement also collapsed, dropping Ben and the gang leader into the arms of the police below.

Commercial High School - Class of 1939.

Manuel G. Batshaw.

MANUEL G. BATSHAW

Manny Batshaw is in his seventh decade as a social worker—and still going strong. Ask him how he is doing and his answer is inevitably, "Great," delivered with the same vigour as the tiger in the gasoline commercial.

And this determination has informed his long and distinguished career—extending from service in World War II, through community executive positions in the United States and Canada, to heading up a provincial body (the Batshaw Comission) that shaped how young offenders were treated in Quebec, to serving in a multitude of ways as a community fund-raiser and as an advisor.

It is no accident that Manny is the only community professional ever awarded Montreal Jewry's most prestigious award—the Bronfman Medal.

He studied at Queen's, McGill and Western Reserve Universities before undertaking a career in social work which took him away from Montreal. In the United States, he held a national position (as Director of Program and Research for the National Jewish Welfare Board) until old friends—Gordon Brown and Boris G. Levine—pressed him to return to his native city and head up the Federation.

For 12 outstanding years he was at the helm of Federation—then known as Allied Jewish Community Services—and that period became widely known as "The Batshaw Era."

Major changes occurred in the community. The modern headquarters for Federation, Cummings House, was built; the Golden Age Centre nearby became a reality; Caldwell Terrace Apartments, providing dignified housing for low-income seniors, was constructed (most of those who first moved into the apartments were survivors of the Holocaust or refugees from the Hungarian Revolution of 1956).

One of the highlights of Manny's career occurred because of a newspaper article describing how young people were living in difficult conditions under the existing system. Manny formed the Batshaw Committee in 1975 and, after studying the problems in 60 adolescent centres, submitted to the government an 11-volume report still in use that proposed a wide-ranging revamp. The government was sufficiently impressed with the 168 recommendations that it named its new and modified child care centres in honour of Mr. Batshaw.

In earlier years, he was Captain Manuel Batshaw, in charge of social work services for Military District #4, comprising the entire province other than the Quebec City area. His staff provided services to military personnel, and their families.

The positions he has held relative to his profession reflect the esteem in which he is held:

President of the Montreal Branch of the National Association of Social Workers;

President (1962-1964) of the National Association of Community Centre Workers in Canada and the United States;

He received Canada's high honour, the Order of Canada, in 2004;

Nine years earlier, he had become a Chevalier de l'Ordre national du Québec;

Federation Montreal created the position Honourary Executive Vice-President in 1995 to acknowledge his contributions to community;

The Congregation Shaar Hashomayim named him Hattan Torah, the highest award to a congregant for exceptional leadership;

The Jewish National Fund chose him as its Negev Dinner honoree—an exceptional honour for a professional leader. This reflected his lifelong interest in and support for Israel. In fact, a park and a lake in Yeruham, Israel, are named for him in recognition of his work on behalf of Israeli development towns.

His personal life has been equally fulfilling: Manny Batshaw married a social worker—Rachel Levine—in 1940, and they marked their 50th anniversary before her death in 1990.

At present, he is married to a long-time community leader, Ruth Heller Schleien.

His son, Mark, is Chairman of Pediatrics at the National Children's Hospital in Philadelphia; he has, to date, eight grandchildren and two great-grandchildren.

Issie Baum

Issie (Isadore) Baum looks like a Biblical prophet, with his white beard and fervent attitude towards life and the Jewish people. And few people have soaked up the immense amount of knowledge he has accumulated in some 60 years. He once aspired to be a rabbi and he studied at Montreal's Lubavitcher Yeshiva for nearly 12 years—until he was 18, when he stepped away from rabbinical studies and turned to accounting. Nevertheless, the time spent in the Yeshiva heightened his ability to work in his chosen fields of Judaica and Hebraica.

During much of his working life, Issie was the financial accounting manager for a large importer in Montreal. But, after he tucked away his work binders at 5 p.m., another Issie Baum emerged—and, since his "retirement", that is how he is best known.

Isadore Baum became a world-class expert on Judaica and Hebraica with a focus on documents, antique prints and maps and, particularly, philately.

Issie believes—and a lot of people would agree with him—that stamp collecting is the road to an incredible amount of knowledge. "Almost every topic: people, science, arts, literature, sports, diplomacy, history and geography can be found in philatelic Judaica."

Living in the Montreal suburb of Chomedey, Issie and his Israeli-born wife Zila reside in a home crammed with the visual and textual documentation of Jewish history.

Now working through the Internet, he spans the globe (seated in a comfortable chair)—buying and selling items. He has customers, at last count, in 25 countries. And he is equipped with the language skills to relate to people, whether they are buying or selling. His fluency in English, French, Hebrew, German and Yiddish opens many doors for him.

Issie Baum

What were some of the rare items passing through his hands? "I had a letter from Theodor Herzl signed in Yiddish. Usually, he signed in German."

Another very rare piece of history he had was a letter from David Ben-Gurion, founding Prime Minister of Israel, to the then-Golda Meirson, suggesting that the future Prime Minister change her name to Golda Meir.

On one occasion, he owned the original map of the city of Tel Aviv—drawn on a piece of cloth in 1906. In the field of stamp-collecting, Issie strove to add to the historic value of items by having signatures on them. His greatest coup was obtaining signatures on a cover (which he designed himself) on the issue marking the historic meeting of President Carter, Israeli Prime Minister Menachem Begin and Egyptian President Anwar Sadat.

He was able to arrange for Sadat to sign eight, Begin to autograph five (although he had become a recluse by that time) and—finally—to obtain the signature of Carter (peeved that he did not share in the Nobel Peace Prize) on only one! He therefore had one cover with the signatures of all three leaders. It sold for $4,000 US!

Born in Montreal, Issie Baum dropped out of the Accounting course at Sir George Williams University to spend seven years in Israel. Part of the time, he worked as an accountant, part was spent working in the Museum of Antiquities in Tel Aviv/Jaffa.

He had and has a continuing interest in Biblical archaeology. He also, during his stay in Israel, donned a uniform and fought in the momentous Six Day War.

Back in Montreal, he became interested in prints and maps through Joe King, President-Emeritus of the Montreal Print Collectors' Society, and—in his usual intensive way—became an authority in both. For years, he journeyed the world—attending shows where he could meet people interested in his fields. Periodically, he would research and write catalogues which themselves became collectibles. With the increased use of the Internet, Issie sold his van and reaches out world-wide from his computer keyboard, rather than packing up stock and journeying to destinations on three continents as he had been doing. His home office is crammed with an accumulation of precious items discovered over a period of nearly three decades.

Now, if you want to reach Issie, you simply go to judaicasales.com.

Lawrence S. Bergman

Quebec Minister of Revenue
Member of the National Assembly for D'Arcy McGee

Lawrence S. Bergman is a native Montrealer, born December 6, 1940. He obtained his Bachelor of Arts degree from Sir George Williams University in 1961. In 1964, he earned his Law degree from the Université de Montréal, and was admitted to the Board of Notaries the following year. Until 1966, he practised as a notary with a firm before becoming a partner in Berger and Bergman, Notaries, remaining with them until 1994.

For three years, he served on the disciplinary committee of the Board of Notaries.

He was President of the B'nai Brith Bonaventure Lodge No. 2401, 1969-1970. And he was elected Vice-President of the Adath Israel Poale Zion Congregation, 1992-1996, and also a member of the Board of the House of Israel Synagogue in Ste-Agathe-des-Monts.

From 1995-1997, he was Honorary President of the YM-YWHA—Montreal Jewish Community Centres. Mr. Bergman is also a member of the board of the Canadian Institute of Jewish Research.

On October 30, 1996, the Emunah Women of Canada awarded Mr. Bergman the Rabbinat Sarah Herzog Award in recognition of his services to the Jewish Community and the State of Israel.

Since 1998, he has been a member of the Advisory Council of the Faculty of Religious Studies at McGill University, a member of the Montreal executive of State of Israel Bonds, and an honorary director of Canadian Magen David Adom for Israel.

Quebec Revenue Minister Lawrence S. Bergman.

He was elected member of the National Assembly for D'Arcy McGee in the provincial general election of September 12, 1994. He also served as a member of the Education Commission.

On November 2, 1994, he was appointed the critic for the Official Opposition in terms of the application of the Professional Code and Consumer Protection. During this mandate, he also was named a member of the delegation from Quebec to the Ontario-Quebec Parliamentary Association.

He was re-elected to the National Assembly in the election of November 30, 1998, and was on the Education Commission, in addition to his role as critic for the Official Opposition concerning application of the professional code. From April 1, 1999, he has been vice-president of the National Assembly delegation responsible for relations with the Parliament of Central America (PARLACEN), and also a member of the delegation involving relations with Europe (DANRE).

On October 21, 1999, Mr. Bergman introduced Bill 198, an Act to proclaim Holocaust-Yom Hashoah Memorial Day in Quebec. The bill was passed unanimously on December 15.

A month and a day later, on November 22, 1999, Lawrence Bergman was presented with the Jerusalem Award, by the Mayor of Jerusalem, the World Zionist Organization and the Canadian Zionist Federation "in recognition of his outstanding dedication and service to the State of Israel, and the Jewish community."

On June 21, 2000, Mr. Bergman received a medal for Cultural Assistance from the Quebec delegation to "La Renaissance française," an organization under the high patronage of the President of France and Ministries of Foreign Affairs, Interior Defence and National Education.

He was re-elected to the National Assembly in the provincial election of April 14, 2003. Fifteen days later, he was named Provincial Revenue Minister.

EMILE BERLINER

Emile Berliner made the telephone work—not Alexander Graham Bell.
(Canadian Jewish Congress National Archives, Montreal)

Alexander Graham Bell did not invent the telephone. It was actually invented by a Jewish schoolmaster named Johann Phillip Reis. He made the first verified telephone call in 1860. He called his crude device a "telephon." Bell found an example of it in Edinburgh and tinkered with it. But the inventor who turned the instrument from a toy into a working communications device was a sometime Montrealer named Emile Berliner.

Berliner invented the telephone mouthpiece and undulating coil. For a time, the instrument he developed was known as the Bell-Berliner phone.

Berliner also invented the phonograph, the microphone, the flat recording disc (and therefore made possible the entire recording industry), the acoustic tile, possibly the earliest real helicopter, and much more.

He was born in Hanover, Germany, in 1851. Berliner had to drop out of school when he was 14 to help his family.

Working as a clerk in a dry goods store, he designed and constructed a weaving machine.

Later, he was hired to analyze sugar in a laboratory and discovered how to manufacture saccharin from coal tar.

Moving to the United States, he made his inventions to improve the telephone; Bell bought the rights to them.

In 1887, in Montreal, he invented the gramophone, using flat discs whereas Edison, in his talking machine, had used soft wax cylinders for recording.

There is controversy over whether Berliner's helicopter lifted off in 1909 (making it the world's first chopper flight).

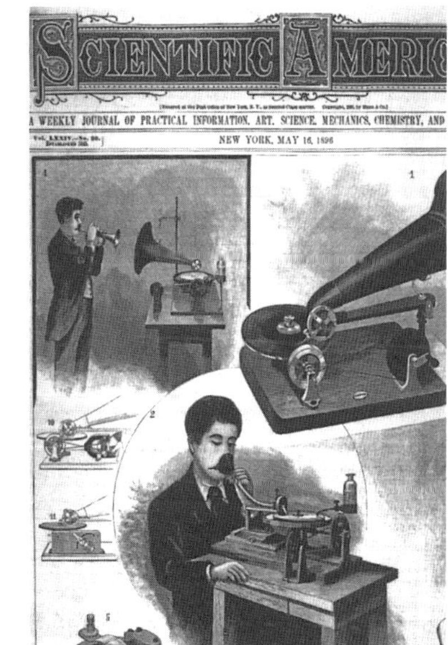

SCIENTIFIC AMERIC

A WEEKLY JOURNAL OF PRACTICAL INFORMATION, ART, SCIENCE, MECHANICS, CHEMISTRY, AND

NEW YORK, MAY 16, 1896

Scientific American, *in 1898, describes Berliner's new gramophone on its front page.*

The Berliner helicopter used a lightweight aircraft engine he designed.

Monty Berger

Monty Berger's life has been shaped by the traditions of his people. The son, grandson and great-grandson of rabbis, he has conducted his life deeply and genuinely concerned for the well-being of his fellow citizens.

Whether it was founding a synagogue (Congregation Beth-El), reshaping an organization to greatly increase its services to families of the mentally ill (Ami-Quebec), or serving as President of the central federation of Montreal's 100,000-member Jewish community, (Federation CJA) Monty's communal career has been characterized by vigour, imagination and creative leadership.

Even in "retirement," he continues to be active, helping to establish the McGill Institute for Learning in Retirement, playing a leading role in Ami-Quebec, Alliance for the Mentally Ill, and providing creative input to the Montreal Jewish Publication Society. His communal career spans more than half a century. Here are some of the highlights:

Monty Berger is presented with the Caring Canadian Award by the Governor General, Adrienne Clarkson, in 2004.

1956-1957 - President, Quebec Society, Canadian Public Relations Society;

1971-1973 - President of Federation/CJA , Montreal, then called Allied Jewish Community Services;

During his Presidency, the Jewish Community Foundation was created (1971); Cummings House, the new Federation headquarters, was completed (1972); Jewish Family Services was created (1972);

A landmark study of Jewish poverty was released (1972);

Caldwell Residences was formed to provide dignified housing for elderly with low income (1973); the Young People's Division was created (1973);

The March to Jerusalem was organized (1973); Space was found for the Holocaust Museum;

1973-1976 - Vice-President, Council of Jewish Federations and Welfare Funds;

1975-1976 - President of the Canadian Club of Montreal;

1980-1981 - President, Toronto Society, Canadian Public Relations Society;

1989-1993 - Study Group moderator since 1989 and Council Member 1991-1993;

1990-1992 - Leadership roles on the Task Force on Federalism;

1990-1993 - President of Ami-Quebec Alliance for the Mentally Ill;

1998-2005 - Senior Advisor to the Montreal Jewish Publication Society.

In the business world, Monty Berger was a distinguished figure in the field of public relations. His company, Berger and Associates Canada Inc., grew to include offices in Montreal, Toronto, Ottawa, Calgary, Vancouver and Edmonton.

During World War II, Monty Berger served as Senior Intelligence Officer of 126 RCAF Spitfire Wing. He was in the advance parties of the wing—the first ground officer to land on the Normandy Beaches at D-Day Plus One, and was in the advance parties establishing 17 air-strips through France, Belgium, Holland and Germany.

His experiences are summarized in his book *Invasions Without Tears.*

Monty Berger was born in Quebec City, in 1918, to Rabbi Julius Berger and Rebecca Fitch. Seven of Monty's antecedents were rabbis.

Monty studied at McGill University (Bachelor's degree, honours in political science and economics, and Columbia in New York (Master's degree in journalism), and prior to the war was a reporter and acting city editor for the *Chronicle-Telegraph* in Quebec City.

He enlisted in the RCAF in May, 1941.

After the war, he returned to his journalism career with the Montreal *Gazette*, and then began his prominent role in public relations. He became involved in community activity when the Jewish Vocational Services were formed in 1945 to help returning veterans.

Monty's first love was a Londoner, Sonia Mindel. He met her in Montreal when she came to visit her sister and family. They were married in 1947 and had three children—Ann, Joy and Eric (who now lives in Israel). Sonia died in 1977.

Monty later married Jean Soloway Levy.

Prof. Lawrence M. Bessner, FCA

"Lawrence Michael Bessner speaking," is the way he answers the telephone, enjoying meeting and chatting with the hundreds of people he has encountered during an active and long life—as an accountant, a university professor and a community leader. He is probably proudest of the hundreds of students who studied commerce in his classes—first at Loyola College and later, when the College merged with Sir George Williams University, at the resultant Concordia University.

In 1993, the University acknowledged its debt to the lanky accountant by naming him its first Professor Emeritus of Accounting.

Bessner graduated from McGill University (1949—Honours B. Comm. in Economics and Political Science), then turned to teaching, in 1951, the first Jewish academic hired by the Roman Catholic Loyola College.

He became Director of the Faculty of Commerce and Acting Chair of the Department of Accounting. From 1963-1975, he was the first Dean of Loyola's Faculty of Commerce.

When the two institutions merged (and he had a hand in that, too), he became Concordia's only full-time professor specializing in taxation. And for close to three years—1980 to 1982—he chaired the University's Department of Accounting.

Forms his own accounting firm

He formed his own accounting firm, which evolved into Bessner, Gallay, Shapira, Kreisman, and he continued, long after his retirement in 1988, to be a senior consultant to the company.

Larry Bessner has been a prominent leader of Jewish affairs for decades.

His links with Israel, for example, include his national presidency of Canadian Friends of Tel Aviv University (which he co-founded with Senator Yoine Goldstein and Meier Segals) and Montreal President of Canadian Friends of Haifa University. Tel Aviv University named its Biology Research Building in his honour, and awarded him an honorary fellowship.

He was a longtime Chairman of Israel Bonds, national treasurer of Bonds for more than a decade, and, furthermore, served as national treasurer for Canadian Jewish Congress.

Born in Montreal in 1921, he was the son of a grocer (Harry)—an immigrant from Austria. He enlisted in the Royal Canadian Air Force early in World War II, married Terry Gittes who was a member of the Women's Division of the Air Force, and returned to civvy street only in 1946.

Lawrence Bessner (centre) flanked by Prime Minister Jean Chretien and Mrs. Chretien.

More than six feet tall, he picked up and retained the airman's swagger, and was readily recognizable at a distance.

"I believe," he once said, "that life is like bookkeeping—a double entry system. You have a choice of giving or taking, and there is much more satisfaction in being a giver rather than a taker."

Marcel Braitstein, R.C.A.

Sculptor/photographer/author Marcel Braitstein has terrible memories as a 7-year-old child being shot at by German soldiers occupying his Belgian home town. The frightening childhood recollections have obviously influenced his work. Yet, in other ways, he tries to turn the page of life—striving to escape the past and live in a happier world.

He is multi-talented—writer, photographer, poet, sculptor and—for 30 years—a professor at the Université du Québec à Montréal.

He lost his family in World War II. From July of 1942, until the end of the war (when he turned 10), a Protestant gentile family hid him. His grandparents survived and he was returned to them, and an aunt, when the conflict ended. His parents had perished in Auschwitz.

In 1951, he came to Canada. He studied at the École des Beaux-arts in Montreal, the Instituto Allende in Mexico and, in Europe, on Canada Council grants, 1961-1964. He began teaching at the Université du Québec à Montréal in 1969, and was visiting professor at Mount Allison University in Sackville, New Brunswick, 1973-1975.

He was director of the Fine Arts Department at UQAM 1986-1991. He retired in 1998.

He used bread in his first attempts at sculpting but later worked in welded steel. When he retired, he and his wife Elaine, a retired art curator, converted the extensive grounds of their Hudson home into a living museum. Braitstein's bold steel sculptures are scattered over the three-acre estate.

A member of the Royal Canadian Academy, his more important commissions have included a Holocaust Memorial sculpture for a synagogue in Sault Ste. Marie, Ontario; a commemorative relief in the Atrium of Alcan House in Montreal, a monument for the Government of Canada of one-time Prime Minister Arthur Meighen and a wall sculpture for the Ministère des Affaires Sociales, installed in Longueuil, Quebec.

Prophet, a steel sculpture by Marcel Braitstein in the Musée du Québec collection.

Rita Briansky

"All her works contain elements of tenderness and poetic sensitivity," a critic for the Montreal *Gazette* wrote about artist Rita Briansky.

Rita was 4 years old when her parents brought her to Canada.

She showed an interest in art at an early age and, in 1941, studied under Alexander Bercovitch, at the Y.M.H.A. A year later, she studied with Jacques de Tonnancour at the Montreal Museum of Fine Arts.

After World War II, she spent two years studying at the Art Students League.

Highly regarded as an artist, Rita surged to special prominence, particularly in 2005. First, the Concert Society of the Jewish People's and Peretz Schools honoured her—the first artist to be so honoured since Louis Muhlstock in 1990.

Rita Briansky was honoured by the JPPS Concert Society. (Heather Solomon photo)

Further, when friends decided to honour community legend Manuel G. Batshaw on his 90th birthday, *The Canadian Jewish News* ran a photo of the Briansky painting he received and Stephen Bronfman, who was the presenter.

Rita Briansky was born in Poland, and her family moved to northern Ontario just as the Great Depression began.

Her father was a shochet and Hebrew teacher, and the family settled in the town of Ansonville, now part of Iroquois Falls.

Times were so tough her mother took in boarders. But Rita showed an early interest in art, and was fascinated by the aurora borealis, and wild flowers.

Moving to Montreal at age 16, she attended art school with Moe Reinblatt and Esther Wertheimer.

Widely recognized for the quality of both her etchings and her generally bright and happy paintings, Briansky was chosen by *Reader's Digest* to have her etchings grace a cover.

After a visit to Nazi death camps, she painted her "Kaddish" series, now on display in the Health Sciences Library of the Jewish General Hospital in Montreal.

For years, she has taught, at both the Visual Arts Centre and Saidye Bronfman Centre School of Fine Arts, and—in recent years—at the Cummings Jewish Centre for Seniors.

SPECIAL for LADIES

The Fall Season is now at hand and we have imoorted the latest patterns and dcoigns frnm New York and Paris. We have a magnificient stock of materials for Costumes and Skirts. A trial order will convince you of our ability to produce perfect fitting garments. Prompt attention and reasonable prices are our specialities.

A. SABBATH,

HigH-Class Ladies' Tailoring,

912 ST. LAWRENCE BLVD.

Two-Gun Cohen

Abraham Morris Cohen was assuredly the most colourful Jewish resident of Montreal. How many Jews do you know who were Generals in the Chinese Army? The answer can be only one: Abraham Morris "Two-Gun" Cohen.

Two-Gun Cohen takes time out to enlist in the Edmonton Irish Guards, during World War I. (City of Edmonton Archives A96-79)

Cohen was the sturdy son of poor Jewish immigrants, born in London in 1889. A husky boy, he got into trouble, aged 10, when the police hauled him in for picking pockets! His parents could not afford to buy enough food to match the huge appetite of their brawny son.

Too young to be jailed, he was put into a newly-established Jewish Industrial School, at Hayes, from which he emerged—educated and well-fed. However, after a spell in a reform school, and a stab at earning a living by boxing, his angry Orthodox parents (on borrowed money) shipped him off to the "Colonies" (that is, Canada) where they hoped the open spaces of the Prairies would help him go straight.

It didn't. In Saskatoon, he tried his hand at a number of things (ranch-hand, real estate speculator, peddler), but ended up as a professional gambler. He was not the type of man to fool with. When two cowboys sneered at him and called him a "dirty Jew," he shot them!

Another turning point in his life came one evening, in 1908, when he entered a Chinese restaurant which had a gambling establishment in the back. He found the aged proprietor, Mah Sam, being held at gunpoint. Cohen wasn't going to let some thug interfere with his plans for a substantial Chinese dinner followed by a few hours at the gaming tables.

"I saw it was a holdup, but I wasn't heeled (didn't have a gun). I closed in 'till I was too near for him to use his rod and socked him on the jaw."

Mah Sam was astounded. A white man had helped an oriental! At this period in Canadian history, anti-oriental feelings were very strong.

Cohen became a hero to the Saskatoon Chinese community. And when the future President of China, Sun Yat Sen, visited Canada to raise funds for his revolutionary Nationalist Party, he was so impressed he hired the gun-slinger to be his bodyguard.

Once wounded in his left arm, Cohen began wearing two pistols—one on his hip and the other, in a holster, on his shoulder—-hence "Two-Gun."

Sun Yat Sen, after a revolution, became President, and he promoted Cohen to the rank of Colonel. The two apparently became very close. They had a number of discussions comparing the Chinese and Jewish people, and the President ultimately presented the Jewish soldier with a letter addressed to all Chinese urging them never to harm a member of the Jewish community. (That letter, in 1947, convinced the Chinese Ambassador to the United Nations to change his stand. He had planned to oppose the plan to partition Palestine and allow the creation of Israel. Instead, China abstained.)

After Sun died, in 1925, Cohen was named a General in the Chinese Army! He was also the only Occidental to be a member of the Kuomintang, the Chinese national political party.

Two-Gun commanded the Chinese 18th Field Army and it is stated that his troops were the most effective fighting force against invading Japanese troops.

Cohen was more than a General. He was a gun-runner for the Chinese, and a spy-master, setting up espionage teams throughout occupied China (he penetrated a major Japanese spy ring in Shanghai and was able to alert the Chinese that Japan planned to invade Manchuria.) From his headquarters in Canton, he handled banking transactions for his patrons and dealt with Western manufacturers of military equipment. He was given wide authority to acquire weapons for the Chinese, including aircraft.

He was so important an advisor to Sun's successor, Chiang Kai Shek, that he was, in effect, functioning as China's Minister of War. However, in 1943, when he slipped into Japanese-held Hong Kong, in an effort to rescue Madame Sun, the Japanese captured him. (Asked why he risked being captured, he replied, "It was the last service I could do for Dr. Sun"). The Japanese hated Cohen particularly because he had let the world know that Tokyo was using poison gas against the Chinese, and had obtained a gas cylinder, with Japanese markings, as proof. They announced plans to behead him, but the British exchanged an important Japanese prisoner to rescue him, after he had been held and tortured for two years. Why such a priority was placed on Cohen has never been explained. It likely was, in part, because of Chinese pressure. However, it is suspected that Cohen, at times, undertook missions for both Britain and the United States, although no details have been released.

The Nationalist Chinese felt he was so loyal that, at one time, he was trusted with the country's gold bullion.

A Canadian Jewish Congress cartoon on the life of Two-Gun Cohen.

He returns to Canada

Having lost almost 100 pounds in Japanese custody, he journeyed to the United States and then to Montreal. The Jewish community was thrilled to meet the one and only Jewish General in the Chinese Army, and Samuel Bronfman set the stage for his year-long stay by organizing a welcome dinner at the Mount Royal Hotel. 500 turned out. And Cohen, now determined to leave his soldier-of-fortune days behind him, married a Montreal girl and tried, with a degree of desperation, to make an honest living.

Once more, it didn't work, and after a year of trying, Cohen felt that he was becoming a parasite, living off his wife's dress business. And he returned to England.

For the rest of his life, he was held in high regard by both Chinese factions—the Communists who seized mainland China in 1949, and the Nationalists, who were confined to the island of Formosa. After the Revolution, Cohen made several visits to China in a vain effort to bring about a reconciliation between the two feuding groups.

There was more to it than that. Sun Yat Sen had mentioned Two-Gun in his will and Cohen made an annual pilgrimage to China to pick up his "pension."

In 1954, a photographer who encountered Cohen in Hong Kong described him with these words:

"He was beefy and tough-looking and his scarred face bore mementos of his prize-fighting days."

Two-Gun died in 1970, in Manchester, where he is buried in the Blakely Jewish Cemetery. And a grateful Madame Sun, widow of the President, personally inscribed a tribute, in Chinese, on his tall, black gravestone.

The Honourable Irwin Cotler

Irwin Cotler has been Member of Parliament for Mount Royal since 1999, and Canada's Justice Minister since 2003.

The Justice Minister was once described by *MacLean's* magazine as "Counsel for the Oppressed," noting that, as an international human rights lawyer, he has provided counsel to some of the most prominent "prisoners of conscience" in modern times. These have included Andre Sakharov in the Soviet Union, Nelson Mandela in South Africa and Jacobo Timmerman in Argentina. More recently, he has fought for the rights of, among other people, Professor Saad Edin Ibrahim, the leading democracy advocate in the Arab world. He has lectured both in Arab countries and Israel for more than 20 years and has also participated in *rapprochement* dialogues between Israelis and Palestinians.

In 1992, he was named an Officer of the Order of Canada for "his extraordinary contribution to the cause of human rights."

He is also the recipient of five honorary degrees.

Gerald Jack Danovitch (1932-1997)

The man with the saxophone

Gerald Danovitch, son of a news vendor, got his start in music studying at Baron Byng High School, and began playing the alto sax when he was 13. Later, he undertook more serious studies with Joseph Moretti and Arthur Romano at the Conservatoire de Musique.

He was awarded the Premier Prix - saxophone (1952) and the same honour, on the clarinet, the following year. He continued to study the clarinet with Prof. Moretti at McGill University but his real love was the saxophone. He founded, in 1968, and led the internationally acclaimed Gerald Danovitch Saxophone Quartet for much of his adult life.

Carl Urquhart wrote in the Montreal *Gazette*:

"If you've ever heard the Gerald Danovitch Saxophone Quartet live then you know that it is one of the best in the business. Through dedication and uncompromising musicianship, the players themselves have helped raise the saxophone to the position of concert hall status that it richly deserves."

One of the most interesting aspects of Gerry's life were the stars with whom he worked, providing background orchestral music for them. The list is a who's who of the stars of the middle of the century. The list includes Bob Hope and Bing Crosby, Frank Sinatra, Judy Garland, Tony Bennett, Danny Kaye, Peggy Lee and Anne Murray.

He began teaching at McGill University in 1964. One-time Dean of Music, Helmut Blume, called him "the father of the jazz program at McGill."

Blume added, "Until 1955, the dean of the faculty was dead set against jazz on campus."And Danovitch was known as a perfectionist. "Once a kid has made it into university, I expect them to learn as fast as professionals."

Danovitch was a natural. He began performing professionally while still a high school student. He played on CBC radio and later, on television.

He was known for the swiftness with which he would learn a score, for flute, clarinet, saxophone or woodwinds.

Too Much Attention

The Jewish General Hospital was opened on October 8, 1934, with one patient and 10 nurses! The nurses were, of course, anxious to please the patient and all fussed about her until finally, she asked to be left alone. Nurse Estelle Frohlich put it this way: "We almost killed the poor woman with kindness. She begged us to leave her alone so that she could sleep."

ROSETTA MAUD ELKIN

Rosetta (nee Wolff) Elkin is a chapter out of Quebec history—a direct descendent of the first Jewish settler in Quebec, Aaron Hart, and with family connections to the Joseph family, pioneers of great significance in the growth and development of Canada.

Rosetta was born in St. Casimir, Quebec, in 1914, daughter of Martin Wolff (a veteran of the Boer War who had come to Montreal, from England, for a visit) and Irene Rachel (Joseph) Wolff. She had five sisters—Annette, Esther (Blaustein), Fanny, Rachel and Sarah.

Rosetta studied at the Macdonald School for Teachers and Queen's University (B.A., 1945), and began a teaching career.

She married F. Victor Elkin, in 1939, and they had four children—Jacob Joseph de Sola, Irene, Douglas Victor and Brahm Andrade. There are 16 grandchildren and four great-grandchildren, to date.

Community involvement was interwoven into her life at an early stage. She was the first woman vice-president of Congregation Shaar Hashomayim, 1969-1972 (her classmate in Westmount High, Mildred Lande, became the first woman president of the Shaar), chaired the Women's Division of Combined Jewish Appeal in 1968, and was the first chair of the Federation's Cultural Services Division (1967-1969). She was also chairman of the Comité de la fait Française (1969-1979). In 1970, she headed up the group studying the Jewish Public Library and the "Elkin Report" mapped major changes in the functioning of the library.

Outside the Jewish community, she was active too—serving as a member of the National Executive of the Girl Guides of Canada, active on the Board of the John Howard Society and a member of the executive (the only Jewish one at that time) of La Federation des Femme du Québec.

With her sisters, she has been active in preserving rich family records, and has written a book based on her mother's diaries.

In 1994, she was presented with Canadian Jewry's highest honour—the Samuel Bronfman Medal.

Aaron Hart, the first permanent Jewish settler in Canada (1760) encouraged his sister—who had married into the Joseph Family—to send her children to this country for which he saw a great future. Henry Joseph, his nephew, arrived in 1789. Many of the Josephs took the name Henry so Annette R. Wolff (b. Montreal, 1911) dubbed him Henry I! He was her great-great-grandfather.

The name Joseph is intertwined into the history of Canada's growth and development as the family initiated the Canadian merchant marine, supported the first railway and pressed for construction of the Lachine Canal.

Jacob Henry Joseph (1814-1907) was a founder and director of the Montreal City and District Savings Bank and the Montreal Street Railway. His brother, Jesse, headed up the horse-drawn street railway (when it was suggested that the street railway be electrified, Jesse—then in his late 80s—snapped "no self-respecting person would ride in a horseless street car.")

Smart Ideals in Tailoring

Your Fall and Winter Clothing Should be Ordered at

WM. N. KARP

39 St. Lawrence Boulevard

FOR MANY YEARS IN NEW YORK I HAVE MADE THE BEST FIFTH AVENUE WORK. MY AID IS TO GIVE MONTREAL THE BENEFIT OF MY EXPERIENCE

Large Range of Cloths and Patterns

Tel. Main 6553

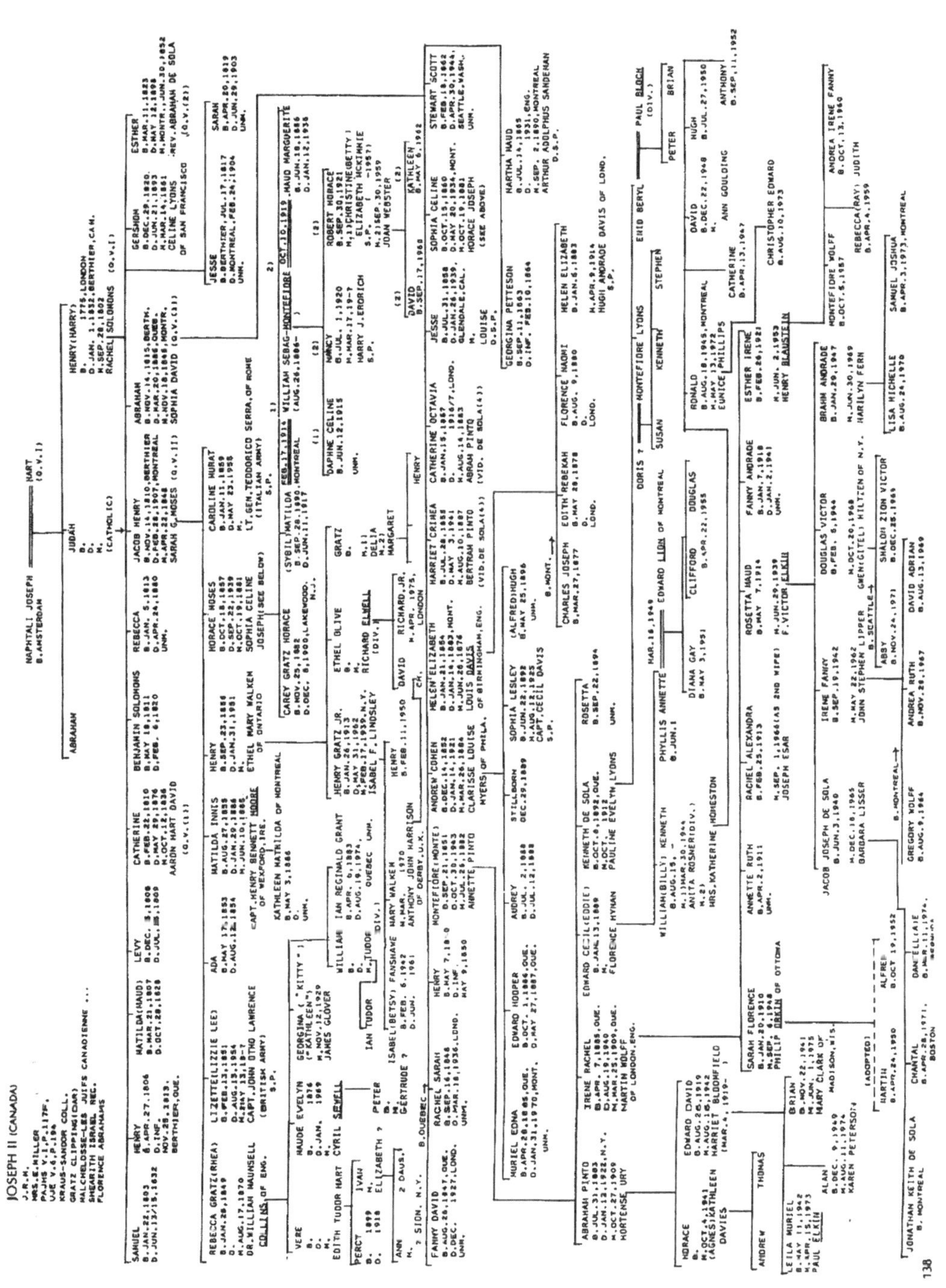

Family Tree of the Joseph Family—one of the earliest and most important Jewish families of Quebec.

Leonard Ellen has been honoured by two universities

Leonard Ellen

Leonard Ellen has held some of the most important community positions in Montreal—the Presidency of both the Sir Mortimer B. Davis Jewish General Hospital and Caldwell Residences. And in the academic world, he is the proud bearer of two Honorary Doctorates—one from Mount Allison University, in Sackville, New Brunswick, and the second from Concordia University, in Montreal.

Furthermore, his name and that of his wife, Bina, adorn Concordia University's Art Gallery which, in the words of the university, "has become a museum of the highest standard, thanks to his (Leonard Ellen's) generosity." The couple is interested largely in Canadian art.

Mr. Ellen's work in earlier times took him into the Maritimes. He became involved in the leadership of Mount Allison University, joining their Board of Regents, and assisting the institution for eight years. Concordia University sought his help and he joined their Board of Governors and, in the mid-1980s, became active in the university's capital campaign. The head of the campaign, Bill Stinson, said that if he had to "single out any one person as responsible for that (campaign) success, it would be Leonard Ellen."

By the late 1980s, he had become chair of the Board's University Advancement Committee.

Enthusiastic and knowledgeable art collectors, Bina and Leonard Ellen then undertook, in 1992, to give the Concordia University Art Gallery a new lease on life. The Gallery was moved to the University's McConnell Building and now bears their name.

In 2000, the university Board of Governors held a special ceremony to honour Leonard Ellen by naming him Governor Emeritus.

Leonard calls the Jewish General Hospital "the greatest gift from the Jewish people to the citizens of Quebec." He was President of the Hospital 1989-1991, after having served from 1982-1986 as President of the Hospital Foundation. The Hospital, he states, is "the flagship of the Jewish community."

He notes that only 27 per cent of those using the Hospital's services are Jewish, so therefore the institution's patients are 73 per cent non-Jewish.

In 1996, the Hospital presented Leonard Ellen with its Distinguished Service Award, and Honourary President Leo Goldfarb commented at the time that Leonard Ellen is "a man of principle, vision and integrity, who devotes his time and energy to the betterment of the community."

Dignified and quiet as he is, Leonard Ellen became a major figure in the Canadian business world. *Quebec Business Magazine* labelled him the "elegant acquisitor."

Working with a Moncton lawyer, Reuben Cohen, he developed a network of financial companies which, in 1988, merged into Central Guaranty Trust, the third largest trust company in Canada.

A native of Montreal, his father was a Russian-Jewish immigrant in the leather goods and aluminum products business. Leonard went out on his own—becoming involved in the lumber business and travelling the Maritime provinces. On one trip, he met Reuben Cohen and they began to make business history together.

Rarely does Leonard Ellen flaunt his wealth—with the exception of his 60th birthday celebration, in 1985. On that very special occasion, he hired the Montreal Symphony Orchestra to play in Place des Arts, and took a crash course so that he, personally, could conduct the Orchestra.

Leonard Ellen married his high school (Strathcona) sweetheart Bina in October, 1945, and celebrated their 60th anniversary in 2005. They have three daughters—Ronna (Mrs. Harry Zelman); Helaine (Mrs. Leonard Kliger) and Sherry. They have six grandsons, one granddaughter and three great-grandchildren.

FEDERATION CJA - AN HISTORICAL PERSPECTIVE

Soon after the first Jews settled in Quebec, the first Hebrew Philanthropic Society was founded. It was established in the spirit of *tzedakah* to give new immigrants to this new land a helping hand and a ready sense of community.

As the Jewish population increased, so did the variety of Jewish institutions. The Jewish Immigration Society was created in 1888 to deal with the influx fleeing persecution in Russia. The great Jewish philanthropist, Baron de Hirsch, made a generous contribution to Montreal's community and had an institute named in his honour that eventually became the cornerstone of Jewish Family Services. In 1903, the Jewish Public Library and Reading Room was formed to cater to the intellectual and cultural needs of the community, and in 1909, the YMHA was opened to respond to its physical needs. In 1917 the newly created Federation of Jewish Philanthropies, the forerunner of today's Federation CJA, ran the first annual campaign to raise money for the gamut of services under its umbrella. It raised an impressive $127,000.

CANADIAN JEWISH CHRONICLE 29

"UNITY IS STRENGTH"

SOME OF THE CAMPAIGNERS FOR $150.000.00 ANNUAL SUBSCRIPTIONS FOR THE FEDERATION OF JEWISH PHILANTHROPIES

(A) Mortimer B. Davis, honorary chairman; (B) Mark Workman, honorary chairman; (C) Garfield A. Berlinsky, executive director. 1, B. J. Hayes; 2, Sol. Z. Fels; 3, Dr. A. P. Ship; 4, I. Lande; 5, I. H. Kaplan; 6, P. Popljger; 7, N. L. Schloman; 8, Wm. Albert; 9, David Blumer; 10, Paul Ogulnik; 11, P. B. Glickman; 12, Fromson; 13, L. Lehrer; 14, M. J. Heillig; 15, I. L. Berman; 16, Max Goldberg; 17, Hiram Levy; 18, Edgar M. Berliner; 19, A. Kellnor; 20, Harry Sessenwein; 21, Dr. E. C. Levine; 22, H. M. Levinoff; 23, J. Elkin; 24, S. Vineberg; 25, T. Glickman; 26, A. Harry Wolfe; 27, H. S. Sourkes; 28, D. M. Chorlton; 29, J. N. Neuman; 30, Sam Holstein; 31, Lawrence Tannenbaum; 32, H. E. Herschorn; 33, Louis Lewis; 34, S. M. Ogulnik; 35, H. M. Levine; 36, A. J. Livinson; 37, A. Rudolph; 38, Douglas Mire; 39, P. Adelstein; 40, Louis Vineberg; 41, B. Rubin; 42, H. N. Friedman, 43, David Kirsch; 44, H. E. Davis; 45, Julius L. Gittleson; 46, A. D. Caltiel; 47, J. Duchow; 48, M. Rittenberg; 49, Louis Vinberg; 50, I. Bald; 51, J. Ginsberg; 52, Alan J. Hart; 53, J. L. Gittleson; 54, Y. Certcoff; 55, C. L. Sommer; 56, L. H. Jacobs; 57, Arthur Schalek; 58, M. Bernstein; 59, S. Moscovitch; 60, A. A. Markus; 61, M. Markus; 62, Mike Bernstein; 63, B. Wilanski; 64, Lionel Coviensky; 65, Abe Rill; 66, David Gordon; 67, C. Feigin; 68, Herman Singer.

The 1917 leadership of Federation CJA

As the community grew, its needs evolved. In 1929 the first Jewish camp came into being in the Laurentians to give children and their mothers respite from the city. In 1931, the Federation added a Women's Division to its campaign, signalling their increasing role in philanthropy and community service. Money was raised to build hospitals to care for the sick and old age homes to ensure shelter for seniors who had to give up their autonomy. Campus Hillel came into being in 1944 as thousands of Jewish war veterans flocked to university in Montreal. That same year, Jewish Vocational Services began helping people find jobs. Six years later, its Sheltered Workshop started training World War II refugees, many of whom were Holocaust survivors, to join the needle trade. Over time, it would become a significant employer of Jews dealing with physical and mental challenges, giving them an opportunity to earn a salary and pursue fulfilling lives.

Federation CJA has kept up with the changing nature of the Jewish community. As more French-speakers from North Africa arrived, the Francophone Sépharade Association was set up in 1966. The renowned Saidye Bronfman Centre opened in 1967 and has become one of Montreal's most notable cultural institutions.

In 1973, the March to Jerusalem was initiated in celebration of Israel's 25th anniversary. This has grown into a much-anticipated annual event and is but one reflection of the community's close attachment to Israel. With the advent of Partnership 2000 in 1995, Montreal was formally twinned with Be'er Sheva and B'nai Shimon in the Negev region.

Jewish schools, being a particularly important outlet for teaching Jewish culture and history, have been integral for continuity from generation to generation and fostering a strong identity. In 1975, the Jewish Education Council of Greater Montreal was formed to coordinate their activities. There are currently 15 individual corporations operating 23 campuses on the island. Their high standard of instruction is ensured by the efforts of the Association of Jewish Day Schools and the Bronfman Jewish Education Centre.

Today, Federation CJA is indisputably the central address for Jewish philanthropy and community service in Montreal. It is responsible for planning and coordinating services for the nearly 93,000 Jews living in the city. The Combined Jewish Appeal is the fundraising arm of the Federation. The proceeds from the annual campaign provide for the most vulnerable Jews in Montreal, in Israel, and around the world. It is one of the 155 North American Jewish Federations and a contributor to the activities of the United Israel Appeal and the Jewish Agency for Israel.

Through its constituent agencies and innovative programs, Federation CJA continues to attend to the health, welfare, social, cultural, educational and recreational needs of the Montreal Jewish community. It provides for the poor, the aged, the isolated, the newcomer, and those facing a myriad of challenges.

FEDERATION PRESIDENTS

Federation of Jewish Philanthropies
1917-1920 Maxwell Goldstein, K.C.
1921-1922 Michael Hirsch
1923-1924 Lyon Cohen
1925-1827 Albert Lesser
1928-1930 Joseph Levinson, Sr.
1931-1933 A.H. Jassby
1933-1950 Samuel Bronfman

FEDERATION OF JEWISH COMMUNITY SERVICES

1950-1953 David Kirsch
1953-1956 Phil Garfinkle
1956-1959 Abe Bronfman
1959-1961 Edward Barkoff
1961-1963 Cecil Usher

ALLIED JEWISH COMMUNITY SERVICES

1963-1965 Lavy M. Becker
1965-1967 Jacob M. Lowy
1967-1969 Gordon Brown
1969-1970 Boris G. Levine
1970-1973 Monty Berger
1973-1975 Charles R. Bronfman
1975-1977 Joe Ain
1977-1979 Hillel Becker
1979-1981 Irving J. Halperin
1981-1983 Dr. Harvey H. Sigman
1983-1985 Dodo Heppner
1985-1987 Carl Laxer
1987-1989 Peter Wolkove
1989-1991 - Dr. Maxine Sigman
1991-1993 Harvey Wolfe
1993-1995 Lester Lazarus
1995-1997 Yoine Goldstein

FEDERATION CJA

1997-1999 Stanley Plotnick
1999-2001 Marilyn Blumer
2001-2003 Stephen Cummings
2003-2005 Sylvain Abitbol
2005- Richard Vineberg

Hon. Sheila Finestone

Sheila Finestone, former legislator, was born in Montreal, Jan. 28, 1927, the daughter of Monroe and Minnie Abbey. She married Alan Finestone June 9, 1947; their children are David, Peter, Maxwell, Stephen. She holds a BS in Edn, McGill U. Among her career milestones: M.P. to House of Commons for Mount Royal, 1984, 1988, 1993-1999; critic for communications and culture, 1985-1993; Secretary of State, Multiculturalism and the Status of Women, 1993-1996; was appointed to the Senate of Canada, 1999;

Advisor to Parliament on eliminating anti-personnel land mines; member, transportation and communication statutes and regulations; vice-chair human rights; member spi. Com. Custody and access in divorce, constitution amendments edcn.; past president, La Fed. des Femmes du Quebec; vice-chair Amendment Equality Rights Can. Constn, 1985; Minister of State Status of Women; leader Cdn. Delegation to Beijing World Conference. On Women's Rights, 1995; mem. Exec. Com. Can. Assn, Former Parliamentarians, Can. Land Mines Found., adopt a Minefield Can. Pres. (hon.) Young Men and Young Women's Hebrew Association; ret. Sec. Parliamentarian Assoc.; v.p. Canadian Museum Of Civilization; Pres. World Exec. Of Inter-Parliamentary Union; mem. Nat. Coun. Jewish Women; hon. Gov. Jewish Gen. Hosp.; mem. Exec. Com. Orgn. Jewish Parliament. Named Person of the Yr. McGill U., 2001. Recipient Jackie Robinson Leadership Award, 1996. Samuel Bronfman Leadership Award, 1995. ORT Sophie Benett award, 1996. Mem. Orgn. Rehab. and Training Liberal.

Kappy Flanders

Kappy Flanders is the Founder and Co-Chairman of the Council on Palliative Care, McGill. The Council's main objective is to promote the understanding of palliative care within and beyond the McGill University Health-Care Network (MUHC). As co-chairman, she has established several lecture series, educational symposia and a website. She has travelled extensively to palliative care congresses nationally and internationally, both to promote the work of the Council and to expand the Council's activities.

In September, 2003, Kappy was awarded the Meritorious Service Medal, by the Governor General of Canada, in recognition of her involvement in establishing the Council on Palliative Care.

In addition to Council involvement, Kappy has participated in the Clinical Integration Task Force of the MUHC and was a member of the Jewish General Hospital Task Force for palliative care.

Kappy Flanders (2nd from r.) with (l. to r.) sister Andrea (Mrs. Charles Bronfman), Israeli Prime Minister Golda Meir, and Kappy's mother.

Kappy is a member of the Canadian Palliative Care Association as well as l'Association Québécoise de Soins Palliatifs. She was a member of the planning committee that formulated the Canadian Palliative Care Initiative, a blueprint to enhance palliative care research, scholarship and care throughout Canada. This working paper was developed in collaboration with senior administrators from Health Canada.

Kappy is a member of the Board of Governors of McGill University. She sits on the committee for the selection of the Dean of Medicine, the Building and Property Committee, the Ad Hoc Advisory Committee on Investment and is chair of the Friends Fund.

She also served a term as a representative to the Senate.

Among the other committees she has served on, are the committees for the selection of the Ombudsman for McGill, the Self Study Task Force (SSTF) for the McGill Medical Faculty accreditation, the Montreal Consortium for Human Rights Advocacy Training (MCHRAT) and the McGill Middle East Program in Civil Society and Peace Building (MMEP).

In 2002, she received an Honorary Life Membership Award from the McGill Alumni Association in recognition of her "support, dedication and enthusiasm" and in May, 2003, she received a "Special Award" from the Alumni Association.

Kappy also sits on the Advisory Board of the Montreal Neurological Institute.

In 2000, Kappy introduced "Mini-Med" to the Faculty of Medicine and was instrumental in in setting it up and running the first series in October 2001. The McGill Mini-Med School, the first of its kind in Canada, is a lecture series, which runs for eight consecutive weeks and is intended to make basic medical sciences more comprehensible to the general public and give them added knowledge. The concept has been a tremendous success in the United States where more than 80 Mini-Med School programs have been offered by medical faculties at universities across the country. In 2003, the Mini-Med School at McGill won the Canadian Council for Advancement in Education (CCAE) Prix D'Excellence Gold Award for Best Community Outreach Program.

Following her husband's death from lung cancer, in 1991, she founded the annual Eric M. Flanders Visiting Professorship Lecture in lung cancer research at the Montreal General Hospital. In 2002, in conjunction with this lecture, Kappy started the Lung Cancer Community Forum, an annual public lecture focusing on the treatment and prevention of lung cancer. In 1994, the Eric M. Flanders Chair in Palliative Medicine at McGill was established in memory of her late husband. Kappy continues to be actively involved in both of these endeavours.

Prior to her interest in palliative care, most of her work was focused on the Jewish community. In 1972, she organized and led the first Women's Mission to Israel. In 1974, she was elected President of the United Israel Appeal of Canada, and in 1973/1974, she was Chairman of Combined Jewish Appeal and National Missions' Chairman. In 1978, she and her family moved to Israel for several years. On her return, in 1981, Kappy organized the vernissage of the Precious Legacy Exhibition at the Montreal Museum of Fine Arts for the Jewish Community Foundation. She was Chairman of the Israel Cancer Research Fund and the Chairman of their Gala fundraising effort.

Kappy was born in London, England, and was educated in England and Switzerland. She was married to Eric Flanders in 1957 and has four children, Susan, Judith, Steven and Ellen. Kappy has lived in several countries and has many interests including art, music, architecture and travel.

PHIL GOLD, CC, OQ, MD, PHD, FRS, FRCP MACP

Phil Gold is the Douglas C. Cameron Professor of Medicine, and Professor of Physioloy and Oncology , at McGill University. He has served as Chairman of the Department of Medicine at McGill and Physician-in-Chief at the Montreal General Hospital. He is presently the Executive Director of the Clinical Research Centre of the McGill University Health Centre.

Dr. Phil Gold

Dr. Gold's early research led to the discovery and definition of the Carcinoembryonic Antigen (CEA), the blood test most frequently used in the diagnosis and management of patients with cancer.

For this work, other studies, and his outstanding contributions as a medical educator, he has gained national and international recognition. He has been elected to numerous prestigious organizations and has been the recipient of such outstanding awards as the

Gairdner Foundation Annual International Award, the Isaak Walton Killam Award in Medicine of the Canada Council, and the National Cancer Institute of Canada R.M. Taylor Medal.

He has been elected to membership in the Royal Society of Canada, the Association of American Physicians, and Mastership in the American College of Physicians.

His outstanding contributions to teaching have been recognized by an award as a Teacher of Distinction from his Faculty of Medicine.

He has been honoured by his country, his province, his city, and his university by appointment as a Companion of the Order of Canada, an Officer of l'Ordre National du Quebec, a member of the Academy of Great Montrealers, and recipient of the Gold Medal of the McGill University Graduates Society, respectively. He has been the Sir Arthur Sims Travelling Professor to the British Commonwealth.

Dr. Gold has been involved in Jewish community functions, at home and abroad, over many years. His major activities have been with the Education Committees and the Boards of various Jewish Day Schools in Montreal. He has often been called upon to speak to Jewish community organizations, on a variety of topics.

Dr. Gold has been married to the former Evelyn Katz since 1960. They have three children—Ian (b. 1962), Josie (b. 1965) and Joel (b. 1968). They also have four grandsons, Zachary, Michael and Benjamin Zeigler; and Alexander Samuel Gold, who are the conjoint apples of their eyes.

Harry Gulkin

Film producer Harry Gulkin is intrigued by the adventure of producing films but his love of Thai food and Thailand itself entangled him in a real-life drama: he narrowly escaped the 2004 Tsunami in south east Asia—hitching a ride on a motorcycle to wind his way up a hill beyond the reach of the killer wave.

Harry is a Montrealer who tried his hand at many ventures before deciding what he really wanted to do with his life—make movies.

His most famous film—*Lies My Father Told Me*—produced in 1975, remains one of the critically acclaimed and successful Canadian films. Two years later he also scored a triumph with *Jacob Two Two Meets the Hooded Fang* based on Mordecai Richler's children's book. He then went on to bring Hugh McLennan's *Two Solitudes* and Chapman Hall's *Bayo* to the screen.

He won a Golden Globe for the Best Foreign film of 1977, for *Lies...* the only Canadian film to win that award to date. His mantelpiece is home to several other awards.

Harry Gulkin did many things before he became intrigued by film-making. He was a portrait photographer (like his father), a merchant seaman, labour organizer (his mother supported the Communist philosophy) journalist, marketing consultant and researcher, and supermarket executive before joining Place Bonaventure, as a marketing and design consultant. This led to his very first film *The Trade Machine*, promoting the downtown shopping facility. The production was chosen as the "best industrial film" at the Chicago Film Festival.

Earlier, while at Steinberg's Limited where he was director of organizational planning and executive assistant to the president, he wrote and co-produced a multi-screen presentation to mark the 70th birthday of Sam Steinberg. Before plunging into feature film production, he produced the documentary *Penny and Ann*. Made for Montreal's Lethbridge Rehabilitation Centre, it picked up several awards, including a second prize at a Tel Aviv film festival.

Harry had acquired the rights for Ted Allan's autobiographical story *Lies My Father Told Me*, and secured Ted's agreement that he write a screenplay. The story about a Yiddish-speaking grandfather, who makes a living collecting rags in the neighbourhood around the Main, and his love for his grandson, took the producer back to his own childhood. "There was a blacksmith at the foot of our yard," he recalls, "who shod the horses of the rag pickers. Every day I saw men like the Zaide in *Lies* and I remember them crying, 'Regs, regs.' "

For years now, Harry Gulkin has worked almost entirely in French, for SODEC which provides financing for Quebec films, helping to determine which films deserve financial assistance. He is especially proud of supporting Denis Arcand's *Jesus of Montreal*, an award-winner at the Cannes International Film Festival, and his *Les Invasions Barbare*, winner of an Oscar in 2005 for Best Foreign Film.

Harry monitored the development of both films, attending all the in-progress screenings and says he was delighted by the awards.

Harry Gulkin, with his varied career, once tried his hand at serving as director of the Saidye Bronfman Centre. But his bold ideas did not sit well and after three and a half years, he stepped down.

His daughter is a highly respected film editor and sometime director based in Toronto. His son, James, settled in Thailand more than two decades ago and exports seafood.

Harry and his wife, Marie Murphy, have vacationed in that country several times—but the Tsunami gave them an experience as unforgettable as the best of the Gulkin films. But Harry still enjoys Thai food, loves to visit his son and plans further vacations in that country.

Hadassah-WIZO Organization of Canada

An Historical Overview

Hadassah-WIZO Organization of Canada (CHW) was founded in 1917 and is a non-political organization dedicated to the support of education, career training, health care, women and youth services in Israel and Canada. HWO is a broad-based membership organization with a multi-layered structure from individual chapters, to Council and City Executive Boards, and ultimately, the National Executive Board. The membership of 15,000 women and 1,100 Male Life Associate members is located in 34 Canadian cities and communities from coast to coast.

For more than 85 years, CHW has been deeply involved with WIZO and this involvement remains steadfast in its dedication and commitment to Israel's women and children. At the same time, for more than 65 years, Canadian Hadassah-WIZO and Youth Aliyah share an unparalleled record of achievement in their commitment to Israel's young people. In addition, Hadassah-WIZO Organization of Canada continues to play an integral role in support of health care services in Israel at Assaf Harofeh Hospital, since 1953, and Hadassah Hospital, since 1991.

To understand the birth of Hadassah-WIZO, we must first look at its growth in the context of the Zionist movement at the turn of this century. Although Zionism originated in Central Eastern Europe in the 1880s, it is actually a continuation of the ancient nationalist attachment of Jewish people to the historical region of Palestine where one of the hills of ancient Jerusalem was called Zion.

Hadassah, in its infancy, functioned as a women's auxiliary or constituent party of the male-dominated Federation of Canadian Zionist Societies founded in 1899. However, it quickly separated itself to become a body devoted to projects that the women themselves selected. They steered their own course early on by formulating their own goals, organizing individual fundraising endeavours and operating from their own national office. Once they officially acquired their separate identity, they continued to serve the Zionist movement—but they served it as women with their own voice and with the emphasis placed on social welfare services on behalf of women and children in Palestine.

Hadassah was the expression of the earliest desire among Canadian Jewish women for an independent forum. It was a vehicle for their Canadianization because their

Lillian Freiman, O.B.E., 1919-1940 · Anna Raginsky, 1941-1947, & Golda Meir · Rosa Singer, 1947-1951, & Vera Weizmann · Sally Gotlieb, 1951-1955, & Eleanor Roosevelt

ottie Riven, 1955-1960, & HRH Queen Mother of Belgium · Nina Cohen, 1960-1964, & Moshe Dayan · Anne Eisenstat, 1964-1968, with David Ben Gurion & Rebecca Sieff · Blanche Wisenthal, 1968-1972, & Levi Eshkol

Neri Bloomfield, 1972-1976, & Golda Meir · Clara Balinsky, 1976-1980, & Menachem Begin · Mirial Small, 1980-1983, & Ephraim Katzir · Cecily Peters, 1983-1987, & Chaim Herzog · Naomi Frankenburg, 1987-1990, & Itzhak Shamir

Esther Matlow, 1990-1993, & Yitzhak Rabin · Judy Mandleman, 1993-1996, & Shimon Peres · Patricia Joy Alpert, 1996-1999, & Ehud Barak · Marion Mayman, 1999-2002, & Ariel Sharon

cultural and social values were shared by their non-Jewish contemporaries. Hadassah served as an entrée into society in both the Jewish and non-Jewish Canadian world, raising its members' profiles as Jews, as Canadians, and above all as WOMEN. Hadassah helped its members define their image to both themselves and to Canadian society as a whole, in ways that reflected their traditional role as caregivers. The energy and emotional commitment of its members was attributable to the Organization's mandate and its appeal to their instincts as women.

As the movement spread across the country, it attracted dynamic leadership from the most prominent people in the communities. Within the Jewish community, the moral influence and political power of the leadership of Hadassah were of such great significance that by the mid-1920s, Hadassah was recognized as the strongest, most coherent and best led organization on the Jewish scene.

In March of 1917, a meeting took place in Toronto that changed the complexion of the women's Zionist movement in Canada forever. On this particular night, Mrs. Anna Selick had arranged for the members of the Beth Zion Synagogue Women's Auxiliary to listen to a guest speaker at her aunt's home that evening.

That speaker was Henrietta Szold.

Mrs. Eva Chait of Montreal was a young girl of 11 years old when she was asked to help out in the kitchen that evening. She recently talked about her memories of what took place. "It was a group that used to come together to sew layettes for unmarried mothers," she recalled, "and Henrietta Szold came to Toronto, and this group was invited to come to my aunt's home where she began to speak about the work for the people in Palestine. She was a very impressive person and the group decided it would form a Hadassah chapter." It was the spirit of Henrietta Szold's speech that motivated them... "It's sort of a spontaneous thing—it bubbles up like you're pouring a glass of champagne. It isn't something that's definitely planned beforehand—maybe Henrietta Szold planned it, but it wasn't planned by those in attendance." Mrs. Chait went on to discuss how Henrietta Szold's visit was just the spark needed to ignite the birth of the Hadassah movement in Canada. "It grew," she said in reference to the organization, following the visit, "in all parts of the city, young people would get together and form a group. It was done on the basis of a group of people who were seeing each other socially and they'd get together, and there probably wouldn't be any more than 16 or 20 to a group."

Some of the women present at that very first meeting became important leaders in Canadian Hadassah in its formative years. Mrs. Selick, for example, went on to become the National Vice-President, then the National President from 1941 to 1947. At the National Convention held in Winnipeg that July, Mrs. Selick, a convention delegate, successfully brought forth a resolution authorizing the formation of Hadassah chapters throughout Canada. Overall, Canadian Hadassah's growth was modest in the first two years with only a handful of chapters concentrated throughout Ontario.

It was at a Zionist convention in 1918 that Mrs. Selick approached Mrs. Lillian Freiman of Ottawa about becoming the first National President of Canadian Hadassah. Respected throughout the nation for her leadership qualities and her devotion to philanthropic endeavours, Lillian Freiman was the logical choice to build Hadassah into a cohesive national Zionist women's organization. On January 19, 19191, Mrs. Freiman was provisionally appointed and later formally elected the first National President of Canadian Hadassah, a position she would hold for over 20 years.

In May 1921, Canadian Hadassah became part of WIZO and from that day onward was known as Canadian Hadassah-WIZO Organization.

Hadassah Centres Coast-to-Coast

British Columbia: Vancouver, Victoria
Alberta: Calgary, Edmonton, Lethbridge, Medicine Hat
Saskatchewan: Regina, Saskatoon.
Manitoba: Winnipeg
Northern Ontario: North Bay, Sault Ste. Marie, Sudbury.
Huron: London, Sarnia, Windsor.
Great Lakes: Brantford, Guelph, Hamilton, Kitchener/Waterloo, Niagara Falls, Oshawa, Peterborough, St. Catharines, Toronto
St. Lawrence Region: Belleville, Cornwall, Kingston, Montreal, Ottawa.
Nova Scotia and Newfoundland: Glace Bay, Halifax, St. John's, Sydney, Yarmouth.
New Brunswick: Fredericton, Moncton, Saint John.

In Israel, Canadian Hadassah-WIZO supports:

Educational projects: social support and career training; Day care centres: a head start for infants and toddlers; Social services projects: responding to diverse needs; Healthcare Projects: Saving Lives.

In Canada, Canadian Hadassah-WIZO supports:

Community building: training today's advocates and tomorrow's leaders; Funding of education; Investing in the future.

Our Affiliations:

Canadian Hadassah-WIZO is affiliated with World WIZO, the Women's International Zionist Organization which has federations in 51 countries on five continents.
Canadian Hadassah-WIZO is affiliated with Hadassah International USA.
Canadian Hadassah-WIZO is the largest constituent organization of the Canadian Zionist Federation.
Canadian Hadassah-WIZO is associated with Canadian Young Judea supporting programming for Jewish youth.
Canadian Hadassah-WIZO is represented on the Executive of the Canadian Jewish Congress.

Rochelle Levinson, National President, CHW, and Shaul Mofaz, Israel Minister of Defense.

Canadian Hadassah-WIZO is affiliated with the National Council of Women of Canada, the United Nations Association of Canada and UNESCO.
Canadian Hadassah-WIZO is a founding member of the Coalition of Jewish Women for the Get—a powerful lobby group fighting for a woman's right to receive a get and an active member of ICAR (International Coalition for Agunah Rights).

Montreal Hadassah-WIZO

Montreal was the acknowledged centre for early Zionist activities in Canada. Women's Zionist groups were formed with the purpose of raising funds to assist women and children in Palestine. In December, 1918, Henrietta Szold visited Montreal and met with representatives of the various women's Zionist groups. She convinced them to restructure themselves into a cohesive Montreal Hadassah organization which would be made up of various chapters. Mrs. Louis Fitch was the motivating force in setting up the Montreal council to coordinate the work done by the city's chapters and she was elected as its first President. Special projects at that time were the Helping Hand Fund and the Magen David Adom.

The dedication and commitment of Montreal Hadassah-WIZO members in assisting women and children in Palestine, and then in Israel, has never wavered. From sacrifice sales to the tremendously popular annual bazaar to the Herman Abramowitz Art Auction, Hadassah Women were always looking for innovative ways to raise funds. In 1950, the Ethel Epstein Ein Chapter compiled a cookbook and reference manual about Jewish holidays and traditions, *A Treasure For My Daughter,* which has become a classic and is still in demand. In 1975, Montreal Hadassah-WIZO joined with their Male Life Associates to hold their first Pro-Am Golf Tournament which recently celebrated its 30th anniversary. Throughout the years, Montreal Hadssah-WIZO has experienced the benefit of strength in numbers, prestige and the concrete results of its efforts.

The Montreal Hadassah-WIZO Council Presidents: Mrs. L. Fitch, Mrs. Louis Miller, Mrs. Rosa Singer, Mrs. J. Cohen, Mrs. William Riven, Mrs. Mary B. Weinstein, Mrs. M. Garfinkle, Mrs. A.D. Paltiel, Mrs. Henry Nathanson, Mrs. A. Slavouski, Mrs. Neri Bloomfield, Mrs. Hyman Heft, Mrs. Myer Sager, Mrs. Sara Policoff, Mrs. Mandy Roskies, Mrs. Miriam Harrow, Mrs. Jeanne Ostrov, Mrs. Shirley Rabinovitch, Dr. Miriam Liberman, Mrs. Ada Morris, Mrs. Irene Mendels, Mrs. Faye Steinfeld, Mrs. Miriam Peletz, Mrs. Yvonne Hardy, Mrs. Diana Shadowitz, Mrs. Ruth Dermer, Mrs. Ellen Smiley, Mrs. Cora Cohen, Mrs. Susan Balinsky, Mrs. Maxine Sanders, Mrs. Sarah Hutman, Mrs. Cookie Epstein, Mrs. Susan Wainberg, Mrs. Renna Bassal, Mrs. Roslyn Joseph, Mrs. Carol Seltzer, Mrs. Lil Goldberg, and Mrs. Harriet Star.

STEFFI AND HARRY HALTON

"His exceptional abilities in aircraft design and development, together with his outstanding personal and leadership qualities have all been of outstanding benefit to Canadian Aviation."

With these words, Harry Halton was inducted into the Canadian Aviation Hall of Fame. And well he should have been. Harry Halton is one of the greatest figures in Canadian aviation history, and quite likely the most important figure in Canadian industrial history.

Born in Pilsen, Czechoslovakia, in 1922, he studied mechanical and electrical engineering in England. After working for a time as Chief Design Engineer for a British firm, he joined Canadair, in Montreal, in 1948.

He worked on, or was responsible for, virtually every design project at this major aircraft manufacturer, but most importantly, while confined to a hospital bed, he was asked to design a wide-body business jet aircraft.

The result was the immensely successful Challenger business jet, sold to companies in the four corners of the earth. And the Challenger design led to the RJ—the Regional Jets.

The Halton designs resulted in billions of dollars in orders for Canadair and its successor company, Bombardier.

On the 20th anniversary of the Challenger's first flight, Bombardier's executive vice-president, John Holding, stated:

"In many ways, the Challenger represents the cornerstone of our aerospace business. The Challenger, quite simply, has been our winning ticket to entering the business and regional aircraft markets—and it's been a winning ticket because it is a marvellous airplane and a true benchmark for the industry."

Incredibly, Harry Halton had achieved this design triumph from a hospital bed. And, for his last years, he remained active—but confined to a wheelchair.

Steffi and Harry Halton. Both born in Czechoslovakia, they met in England.

Often at his side, Steffi Halton was also Czech-born and met her husband-to-be in England, where he managed to get by on 24 cases of Pilsen beer sent weekly to him by his family, prior to the outbreak of World War II.

Both were students, and they married in 1944.

When the couple moved to Montreal, they shared a deep interest in community affairs. Steffi was active in Federation CJA and Temple Emanu-El, and husband Harry become the Congregation president.

The Harry Halton story starts in his native Czechoslovakia where he began his fascination with aircraft. "I wasn't interested in flying them. I just wanted to build them."

His family sent him to London, and safety, shortly before the outbreak of war.

He studied electrical engineering during the day, and worked in a factory at night. The war over, he set up his own design firm, but seeking greater opportunity, he and Steffi moved to Montreal. He joined Canadair, worked on many aircraft designs, but became internationally recognized when he designed a long-range reconnaissance drone. The remote control drone, in use in NATO countries today, is launched from a vehicle and returns to home base, landing with the aid of a parachute.

"It took six years of my life," Halton commented.

Every Monday, Halton flew to the United States Testing Grounds in Arizona, where his CL-289 was being test-launched. He spent the entire week there, rejoining his family (they had three children—Howard, Terrence and Debbie) for the weekend.

With that project completed, his next challenge was to design the first flying boat expressly intended to put out forest fires. The water bomber scoops up 1,200 gallons of water and dumps it on fires. It is used in many countries of the world.

It is, in Halton's own words, "the only flying boat of its kind in the world."

Harry Halton s life almost came to an end on the operating table. He had two major operations on his spine in 12 hours—-and survived. But he was paralysed from the waist down.

The crushed family sat there, and the person who cheered them up was Harry Halton, "It will all be right."

Halton was lying in his hospital bed when the President of Canadair asked him if he would work on the planned wide-body business jet. "Not right now," Halton replied. "I'm busy dying."

But, from a hospital bed, the engineer went to work and the aircraft designers and draftsmen and secretaries came to his bedside to get their instructions.

When the aircraft was completed, Harry—and Steffi—were there, to see their design open a new chapter in aviation history.

The Steffi Halton Page

Steffi Halton wore two pairs of bloomers! She was 12 years old, and the roomy underwear was used by her family to transport valuables as they fled Nazi-dominated Bohemia en route to Gdansk, Poland, and a ship bound for England and freedom.

Steffi's father, Benjamin Apfelbaum, was a self-made man. He started out as a peddler, collecting old clothes. And he became a major manufacturer of textiles. He was also a man with foresight. When his family became endangered in Bohemia, in March, 1939, (he was warned by a friendly Czech Nazi official who advised him that he was on the "black list"!), no one in his family was surprised that he had set up a fully-furnished apartment to shelter them in Prague. Preparing for the second phase of their flight from the Nazis, Bernard Apfelbaum had arranged for a priest to certify they were all good Roman Catholics. The fact that Steffi, and most her family, were blond with blue eyes helped. When Steffi and her father made it to England , after crossing Poland, (her mother and two brothers became separated but ultimately, her mother made it to London via Shanghai, China, while her brothers served in the Royal Air Force), it again came as no surprise that Bernard had taken the precaution, some time before, of transferring a good deal of his assets, from under the shadow of Adolf Hitler, into British banks.

Steffi linked her future with Harry Halton when the two Czech students met in England.

Moving to Canada, while Harry was locked into his challenging work at Canadair, and later Bombardier, Steffi—in addition to raising three children—was busy in several community leadership roles.

Ultimately, she made her mark in four areas:

She was instrumental in merging Temple Beth Sholom , where she served as President of the Congregation, with Temple Emanu-El (where Harry ultimately became President);

She headed up Israel Bonds 1982-1984 and strengthened the organization by recruiting new young leaders;

She was Chairman of the 1972 YM-YWHA Campaign;

And she organized the highly-successful Community Conference "New Horizons", in 1964, which drew 460 participants, and made many more aware of the importance of education.

She was also active in the Combined Jewish Appeal, maintaining a continued relationship with Dodo Heppner and Sheila Finestone.

Hebrew Free Loan Association

"The object of this Society is to loan money to those in need, instead of giving alms, and thus assist respectable people whose character and self-respect will not permit them to receive alms, but who will accept a loan which they can repay and thus overcome the difficulties in their struggle for means livelihood.

"Money is loaned in sums of $5.00 to $100.00, to applicants irrespective of creed, on notes endorsed by responsible people, without charge of interest or expenses of any kind, the borrower repaying the loan in weekly payments"

First Annual Report, 1912, Hebrew Free Loan Association
52 Ontario St. W. Montreal

Fifteen men assembled, in 1911, to create a new organization in Montreal. Zigmond Fineberg was the founding President , and other members of the first leadership team included Moses Albert, Tobias Glickman, Nathan H. Godinsky, Abraham Harris, Archibald H. Jackson, Eli W. Jacobs, Jacob A. Jacobs, Solomon Kellert, Abraham Levin, Manuel Levitt, Hiram Levy, Philip Popliger, Abraham Schacter, and Moses Slabosky

The first year was "difficult, promising", the 75th anniversary report noted, stating the Hebrew Free Loan Association began as the personal project of businessman Zigmond Fineberg. In his travels, Fineberg had seen Free Loans operating in other cities, especially in New York. The Montreal Association was modelled after the New York group and opened for business on September 11, 1911, in quarters owned by Fineberg at 14 Craig Street West.

Starting capital was $6,500. However, Zigmond Fineberg complained that most of the work fell on his shoulders. And an early fund-raising effort—raffling off $100 in gold donated by Mrs. Harris Vineberg—was a failure. For a time, funds were so low that the ceiling for loans was dropped to $50.

However, in the 94 years which have passed since the Hebrew Free Loan was established, the amounts loaned to applicants have risen considerably although the basic philosophy remains unchanged. On its 75th anniversary, the Society commented:

"By making interest-free loans rather than giving handouts, the Association gives deserving recipients the chance to solve their own problems rather than turning them over to the public; and to launch projects that improve the quality of their lives rather than merely holding on to what they have."

The Hebrew Free Loan's presidents:

Zigmond Fineberg, Founder and organizer	1911-1917
Moses Albert	1918-1921
Nathaniel S. Fineberg	1921-1949
William Levy	1949-1970
Joseph Guttman	1970-1974
Joseph Schreter	1974-1977
Louis B. Magil	1977-1980
David Kaufman	1980-1983
Joshua I. Ronn	1983-1987
Arthur Levitt	1987-1989
Bernard Richler	1989-1991
Moses Salzberg	1991-1993
David A. Stein, FCA	1993-1996
Morrie M. Cohen	1996-2000
Mark N. Kraminer	2000-2001
Jack Noodelman	2001-2005
Charles Benisty, CGA	2005-

(The long-time executive director of the Association is Nicky Madoff.)

In 2004, President Jack Noodelman reported that the Hebrew Free Loan, in the previous year, had made 680 loans totalling $2.7-million (an average of just under $4,000 per loan; a far cry from the $5-$100 parameters of 1911!).

The President added, "The loans we have provided respond to needs ranging from education assistance to purchase of a first home to medical expenses, debt consolidation, and so on." It is interesting that the group rarely has a problem collecting a loan.

In 2004, the organization helped people with loans totalling $2,677,982 and reported, for that same period, loan repayments of $2,658, 316.

Donations cover the overhead.

The identity of loan recipients is not disclosed, but, for its 85th anniversary, the Association printed excerpts from several letters, blacking out names of the authors.

The letters tell their own stories... "I send (my first repayment cheque) with my deepest gratitude for your kind assistance, by means of which I could begin a decent life in Canada" ... "The loan has helped a great deal in the present success of my business."... "The loan helped me with basic living expenses while I embarked on a new business."

The Founders of the Hebrew Free Loan in 1911—making up the 1913-14 executive.

As Montreal Campaign Chairman, Tom Hecht (right) donned a flak jacket and experienced the danger of front-line conditions in Israel's fortified Bar-Lev Line.

Thomas Otto Hecht

The road to the Suez Canal that morning in 1970 was pockmarked with shell-holes.

The driver of the Israeli jeep sped along, dodging the gaping holes torn out of the highway until, finally, with a sigh of relief, he swung his vehicle into a shelter at the Bar-Lev Line—the Israeli fortified position on the east bank of the Suez Canal.

Thomas O. Hecht, General Chairman of the 1970 Combined Jewish Appeal of Montreal, had decided he had to know the whole story. Therefore, he commissioned a flight to the very front line of Israeli positions, despite the occasional burst of shellfire, and the crackle of sniper fire, from the Egyptian-held side of the Canal.

It wasn't the first time Tom Hecht had been under fire. The first time was at age 11 when he became separated from his parents and sister in a railway station in France, as German bombers attacked the area. Frightened, he hid under a bench in the station waiting room.

Thomas Otto Hecht was born in Czechoslovakia, in 1929, and with the outbreak of the Second World War—he and his family had to flee the advancing Nazis, somehow finding their way across war torn Europe, reaching neutral Lisbon, Portugal, early in 1941.

After tense months of agonized waiting, they managed to book passage aboard a rusted, overcrowded vessel, bound for Casablanca (to pick up even more passengers), Mexico and, ultimately, New York. It was a voyage aboard a dangerously overloaded vessel, on which smallpox broke out. The ship successfully eluded German U-boats, and flew a yellow flag when it reached Mexico to warn of the contagious disease aboard.

Tom Hecht confers with Israeli Prime Minister Menachem Begin.

On arrival in New York, the family was unceremoniously bundled off to Ellis Island and—alighting from a sealed train in Montreal on New Year's Eve, 1942—were strangers in their new land.

In the wake of the Second World War, the fervently Zionist Tom Hecht—aged 19—journeyed back to Czechoslovakia to train with Irgun Zvei Leumi, the Jewish underground movement. But Tom's father convinced him to return to Montreal rather than get involved in para-military efforts to bring about the rebirth of Israel.

About the same time, the teen-age Hecht had his first encounter with David Ben-Gurion, founding Prime Minister of Israel, in Montreal.

They would meet again, in 1969—this time when Tom visited the Israeli leader at his book-filled hut at the Sde Bker kibbutz in the Negev Desert.

After studying at Concordia and McGill Universities, Tom Hecht pursued an academic career—lecturing, for nine years, at Concordia University in the field of international relations, political philosophy and comparative government.

Tom Hecht (right) with U.S. Secretary of State Henry Kissinger (centre), and Charles Bronfman, in Washington.

His academic background equipped him to serve the Jewish community in general, and Israel in particular, as a valuable advisor, and a capable spokesman. Their association was very close; Tom Hecht regarded Begin as a mentor. The relationship was anything but a one-way street.

However, in 1956, Tom joined the family's pharmaceutical company and, under his direction, the company and successor organizations became major players in the world's plasma- based health care industry.

He first became involved in the community, logically enough, in health care—assuming the Presidency of the Herzl Health Centre, Canada's first preventative health care agency.

In 1970, he was the youngest General Chairman of the Combined Jewish Appeal—the community's most onerous volunteer task.

Thomas Hecht speaks to a Washington Conference, in 1982. Ariel Sharon is on his right.

In 1973, when the Yom Kippur War erupted, Tom Hecht (as President of the United Israel Appeal of Canada) was this country's representative, at a crucial moment in modern Israeli history, on the Board of Governors of the Jewish Agency. The insights he provided to critical meetings reflected his immense knowledge of Israel's circumstances.

In 1978, he was awarded the Herzl Prize for "dedicated service on behalf of the State of Israel."

For five years in the 1980s, he was President of Israel Bonds, in Canada. In 1987, the Montreal Jewish community presented him with its highest honour—the Samuel Bronfman Medal.

Tom Hecht with Quebec Premier Lucien Bouchard. He was the first non-francophone since Eric Kierans, to move influentially in the highest circles of the Parti Québécois administration.

In 1993, he founded the Begin-Sadat Centre for Strategic Studies at Bar-Ilan University, a think tank focused on security issues. Through conferences, symposia and study papers, it has been an important factor in heightening the understanding of complicated Middle East issues. Tom Hecht was the head of the Canada-Israel Committee for a decade and a half, developing strategies for explaining Israel's position to Canadians.

In both positions, he conferred with Israelis at the highest level.

With his six languages and a powerful and passionate speaking style, Tom has been a strong ambassador for the Jewish community in relating to sister communities.

His greatest breakthrough came when he was named to the Board of Directors of the Caisse de dépôt et placement du Québec, Canada's largest private sector investment organization, and the managing authority for Quebec's pension and insurance plans.

He was awarded the prestigious Jerusalem Prize in 1998 for his efforts in "the cause of peace, ecumenism and the unity of Jerusalem." And he was named Chevalier of the Order of the Pleiade in 2001.

The Star of David in a Montreal Church

There is a Star of David in the huge stained-glass window of the Church of St. Andrew and St. Paul, on Sherbrooke Street. The Jewish emblem, in what is known as the "Black Watch Window", honours the courage of a Jewish officer of the 42nd Battalion of the Black Watch in World War I. Lieutenant Myer T. Cohen, who was decorated with the Military Cross, was affectionately known in the regiment as "MacCohen." And it was official. After one penetration of enemy lines, the commander of the 7th Canadian Infantry Brigade, Brigadier A.C. Macdonnell, wrote the unit:

"Well done, 42nd; well done, old Cohen. I herewith and hereby confer on him the brevet rank of "Mac" to be used whenever and wherever he likes, but it must always be MacCohen in the kilt. I am generally pleased and proud of MacCohen and not for the first time."

MacCohen's final action came on November 3, 1917, when he led his unit in an attack on an enemy position at Passchendaele. The highlanders attained their objective—the ruins of Graf House—but when reinforcements were unable to reach them, they held the position until all had fallen.

When the Black Watch Window was being designed, it was generally agreed that Lieutenant Myer T. "Mac" Cohen should have an honoured place on it.

Sam Bronfman and his Ginger Beer

Sam Bronfman never forgot that—at age 5—children in a Manitoba school laughed at the fact that he had to attend school in rags. His family was desperately poor. Ultimately, as head of Seagram's Distillers, he became one of the richest men in Canada. However, the humiliation of the classroom remained with him, so he remained frugal, in many ways, all his life. Every day at 5 p.m., when his offices in a mock Scottish castle on Peel Street were closing, he would go from floor to floor turning off the lights. "Mr. Sam" had the same secretary for more than 50 years and, when he was 80, the two of them tottered around the office—well aware of the other's way of functioning. For Sam, that included a tot of gin every morning at 11 a.m. Promptly at that hour, his secretary would ask, "What kind of mix do you want today, Mr. Sam?" and the liquor magnate would choose his mix of the day. A secretary would be dispatched, and the drink made from a bottle in Mr. Sam's private, locked liquor cabinet. But, late in life, Sam Bronfman was working in the office on a Saturday—which he rarely did. He had no secretary and, worse, no key to his own liquor cabinet. Distraught, he wandered down the empty halls of the castle until he discovered that one of his vice-presidents, Mike McCormick, was in his office, holding a meeting. "I own more booze than anybody in the world," Sam bellowed, "but I don't have a key to my own liquor cabinet." "I'll be through in a few minutes," soothed Mike who shortly thereafter, went down to the Seagram liquor vault where he signed out a bottle of gin. (Because the price of liquor included mostly taxes, a strict inventory had to be kept.) "What kind of mix do you want?" Mike asked his boss. After pondering this immensely important question for a moment, Sam responded, "Schweppes ginger beer." McCormick sent a secretary out for two bottles of ginger beer, and settled down to share a quiet moment with Sam Bronfman. "Do you know, Mr. Sam," Mike noted, making conversation, "Schweppes makes more money out of this drink than we do out of our booze. It's 65 cents a bottle." "What?" responded Sam—quite put out that the soft drink manufacturer was making more money per bottle than he was. A few minutes later, Sam—wanting a second drink—called in a secretary to bring more ginger beer. "But only one bottle this time," he declared, "It's 65 cents!"

BONDS ARE THE BACKBONE OF ISRAEL'S ECONOMIC GROWTH

Over 15,000 Montrealers attended the first Israel Bond "Big Show" June 15, 1953 at the Montreal Forum.

"Jews have come full circle", *Canadian Jewish Chronicle* editorial

"TWO THOUSAND YEARS AGO, TWENTY THOUSAND JEWS APPEARED AS PRISONERS IN THE ROMAN FORUM TO PERFORM SLAVE LABOUR. NOW, A SIMILAR NUMBER, NOT IN BONDAGE, APPEAR AS FREE MEN IN THE MONTREAL FORUM TO CELEBRATE BOND SALES FOR THE DEVELOPMENT OF A NATION."

* ALBEN BARKLEY, former vice-President of the United States was Guest Speaker; and entertainers included violinist Mischa Elman, tenor Richard Tucker, Israeli pianist Menachem Pressler and the Canadian Grenadier Guards Band.

* VARIOUS FUNCTIONS preceding the Montreal "Big Show" included a Mount Royal Lodge, B'nai Brith Reception featuring Franklin D. Roosevelt Jr. as guest speaker and Mrs. S. Frank, Leon Crestohl, Julius Briskin, Samuel Moskovitch, Jan Bart, Isadore Namerow, and Israel Consul- General Yosef Nevo, as Head Table Guests.

* MONTREAL MAYOR Camilien Houde crowned Anne Rottermund as "Miss Israel Bond" in a contest of Jewish Women's Organizations.

* COMEDIAN GEORGE JESSEL distributed Israel Bond Canvasser Kits to volunteer workers of Montreal Hadassah, ORT, Pioneer Women, B'nai Brith, Mizrachi, Synagogue and Temple Sisterhoods.

* IN RESPONSE to an appeal by Israel's Rabbi Isaac Hertzog that "Jews everywhere should conduct a Shavuoth Yizkor Appeal for Bonds", Rabbi S. M. Zambrowsky, Executive President of Mizrachi, asked Montreal Synagogues for their support. B'nai Jacob, Adath Israel, Beth David, Beth Zion of Verdun, Spanish & Portuguese and Young Israel were among the first to agree.

* RABBI HERTZOG emphasized that STATE OF ISRAEL BONDS would help the redemption of Israel and echo "the living truth of the providence of G-d."

In those first three years, 1953-55, Montreal raised $3.5 million (U.S.) for Israel; a sum unmatched in North American cities of comparable Jewish populations.

www.israelbonds.ca

THE JEWISH REHABILITATION HOSPITAL

The Jewish Rehabilitation Hospital was born over 45 years ago out of the efforts of a group of community-minded individuals seeking to offer an environment in accordance with their culture and tradition. The Jewish Convalescent Centre began as a place where their fellow citizens could regain strength after surgery, a heart attack or a stroke.

In 1955, the founders of the Jewish Convalescent Centre raised the necessary funds to purchase a house at 3100 Lévesque Boulevard in Chomedey, which was then converted to care for 15 convalescent patients.

In 1962, the Jewish Convalescent Centre purchased a second house across the road as a 15-bed annex and changed its name to the Jewish Convalescent Hospital, thus doubling its capacity from 15 to 30 beds.

The Hospital first was housed in a Chomedey home.

In the spring of 1964, the Jewish Convalescent Hospital began the construction of a new building. It opened its doors on April 3, 1966, with a 120-bed capacity. This step was a turning point, marking the beginning of an era of professional care and expertise that would become the institution's hallmark.

In 1988, the hospital changed its name to the Jewish REHABILITATION Hospital to reflect the evolution of its expertise, role and mission. Specialized in the field of rehabilitation medicine, the Jewish Rehabilitation Hospital is an acute care hospital centre affiliated with McGill University.

The Modern Jewish Rehabilitation Hospital.

As the Regional Centre for rehabilitation services in Laval, the Jewish Rehabilitation Hospital's mandate involves the dispensation and coordination of the best possible quality of patient care for its clientele. Multidisciplinary teams that share a fundamental goal offer services to maximize the individual's level of functional autonomy. A program of physical rehabilitation interventions and social and professional reintegration is developed for each patient.

In October, 1995, the Jewish Rehabilitation Hospital inaugurated its new Sandra and Leo Kolber pavilion. The expansion of the JRH's physical space allowed for the creation of an outpatient department in order to meet the needs of a growing patient population.

The JRH has committed itself to reducing the incapacities of the physically disabled, to cultivating their compensatory capabilities and to reducing the impact of their disability in the different aspects of their lives. The Hospital is dedicated to adopting a client-centred approach based on the unique needs of each individual patient.

Thanks to its many specialized rehabilitation programs and services, some deemed "national" in scope, the Hospital is a recognized Centre of Excellence in rehabilitation medicine. Dedicated to its mission and committed to teaching and research in a clinical environment, the JRH has evolved into an innovative, state-of-the-art hospital centre confirmed in its role as a scientific and clinical leader in its field of rehabilitation.

Presidents:

1956-1958—Samuel Berenbaum
1958-1959—Morris Cooperberg
1959-1966—Moe Kanisberg
1966-1968—Ben Chazanoff
1968-1970—J.A. Lyone Heppner
1970-1971—Marvin Corber
1971-1973—Stanley Hyman
1973-1975—Ab Robins
1975-1977—N. Murray Koffler
1977-1979—George Reinhart
1979-1981—Carl Charlap
1981-1983—Henry Gittelman
1983-1985—Arnold Shostack
1985-1987—Norman Bercovitch
1987-1989—Grace Alter
1989-1992—Robert Klein
1992-1995—Gerald Stotland
1995-1998—Andre Ibghy
1998-2001—Samuel J. Frishman
2001-2003—Ralph Bienstock
2003-2005—Michael Greenberg

Directors-General:

1966-1971—George Riesz
1971-1974—Morris Jesion
1975-1976—Dr. Nathan Heller (interim)
1976-1980—Alan Peres
1980-1982—Dr. Israel Shragovitch (interim)
1982-1991—Jacques Hendlisz
1991-1995—Dr. Henry Coopersmith
1995-1997—Roslyn Cabot
1997-2005—Andre Ibghy

Foundation Presidents:

1978-1981—Ab Robins
1982-1983—George Reinhart
1983-1984—Carl Charlap
1986-1991—Arnold Shostak
1991-1994—Lynne Kassie
1994-1997 Issie Wiseman
1997-1999—Arthur Diamond
1999-2001—Etty Bienstock
2001-2003—Michael Feil
2003-2005 –George Reinhart

Joe King

The fact that he is an honorary member of the crew of the U.S. submarine "Halfbeak," has met and interviewed virtually every major leader in the history of modern Israel, spent half a day travelling with the lanky French President, General Charles de Gaulle, produced a television documentary with the first human in space, Yuri Gagarin, has been called "historian of Montreal Jewry," and is known as an impassioned speaker on behalf of Jewish causes, gives some idea of the many dimensions of author/journalist/broadcaster Joe King.

Joe King, holding the CJCH microphone, in a scrum with Soviet Cosmonaut Yuri Gagarin. Later, King and Gagarin dined with American railroad owner Cyrus Eaton, and a KGB agent (Soviet Secret Service).

Joe became involved in journalism, in his native Toronto, as a copy boy with The Canadian Press News Agency—a much sought-after position, and training ground, from which have emerged some of Canada's greatest journalists. It took him all of six weeks to get promoted and earn a raise, coupled with his joining the staff of the agency's brand-new radio division, Press News Limited (PN). He became a pioneer in the field of radio news.

Supervision editor at 23

He served in the Royal Canadian Air Force in World War II (attaining the rank of Pilot Officer), then returned to Toronto, and, at 23, became the agency's youngest senior editor.

Joe King, left, profiling Canadian Prime Minister Lester B. Pearson.

In 1960, Joe became a co-founder and ultimately Vice-President, News and Public Affairs of the CTV television station, CJCH, in Halifax. At that station, he won the Liberty Television

Documentary Award with a program on Adolf Eichmann and the Holocaust. And Dalhousie University in Halifax awarded him its prestigious Golden "D".

Hosting an hour-long news and public affairs program five nights a week, he also produced documentaries (the one with Yuri Gagarin was called *Cosmonaut and Capitalist*, and also featured Canadian/American industrialist Cyrus Eaton).

His series of TV profiles included Prime Ministers Lester B. Pearson and John Diefenbaker.

His biggest newsbreak in Halifax was a world beat on the loss of the U.S. submarine "Thresher". A Royal Navy submariner (the R.N. still had a Halifax base in the 1960s) tipped the newsroom off.

Moving to Montreal

Joe King, wife Shandle Lipkus, and their three children (Howard, Barbara and Norman) moved to Montreal in 1966 and Joe joined the staff of CFCF Radio and Television (Channel 12), producing and hosting more award-winning documentaries. He won Radio and Television News Director Awards for *Cry of a Child*, the story of the Montreal Children's Hospital, and *Vimy*, the great victory for Canadians in World War I. His interviews with survivors of that battle were among the last for the aging warriors.

He undertook many programs on Canada's armed forces. The most important were his documentary *Bonaventure* on the Canadian aircraft carrier, and *Hunt and Kill*, shown seven times on the CTV network.

For *Hunt and Kill*, King and his cameraman, Tom Cahill, took off from an aircraft carrier (an interesting experience; the speed of the vessel plus the wind speed coupled with the velocity of the plane thrust off the deck by a launching device, must add up to a number sufficient to make the aircraft fly. Otherwise, you plunge into the drink. As this was in the Caribbean where it is always meal-time for sharks, the navy was kind enough to provide its passengers with shark repellent).

Other interesting experiences were being lowered from a helicopter to the swaying deck of a submarine encircled by sharks' fins, and using a cable for a transfer, at sea, from one vessel to another.

The Bluenose

On another occasion, Joe King met with William James Roue, designer of the famous Canadian racing schooner "Bluenose" (the vessel on the Canadian dime).

Mr. Roue loaned King the original blueprints for the craft. Asked why Bluenose outraced all opponents, the designer suggested it was because he raised the bow of the schooner to make it more comfortable for the crew. "That meant the prow of the ship knifed through the water rather than nosing into the waves."

In June 1967, Joe made the first of 19 visits to Israel—sent by CFCF Radio and Television to cover the Six Day War. On his return, as a gift to the Combined Jewish Appeal, he wrote, produced and narrated a Big Screen called *After the Storm*, on Israel in the wake of its stunning victory over the Arab armies—but with emphasis on the human cost.

King with Israeli General Moishe Dayan (with the eye patch). Others in the picture include Thomas Otto Hecht (left) and Gordon Brown.

Joe King and the Israeli general had a standing joke about who gave the orders. "Remember," Dayan would insist laughingly, "I'm the General, you're not the General." Nevertheless, King would continue to give General Dayan orders about what he wanted him to do and the General, like a good soldier, would obey.

This picture is unique in that it is the only one known to show an Israeli secret service agent (the chap in the dark glasses in the background) smiling!

In 1969, responding to an invitation from Federation President Gordon Brown, he joined Federation CJA for a 20-year stint as Director of Communications.

For the Federation, he conceived and wrote a variety of publications, wrote histories of the community for CFCF-12 and the Canadian Broadcasting Corporation.

"Retirement"

Despite a rather substantial vocabulary, Joe King doesn't understand the meaning of the word "retirement."

After stepping down from his communal post, King's activities have included working with his friend A. MacKenzie Brockman on an art and antique house they called MacKenzie-King; he served as Associate Editor of Montreal's *Senior Times* (a paper which continues to carry his views), spent six years as Executive Director of Canadian Friends of Tel Aviv University before switching, in 2000, at the invitation of his friend Morley M. Cohen, to become Executive Director of Canadian Friends of Haifa University.

In addition, King is Executive Secretary of the Montreal Jewish Publication Society which has published a number of his books, including *From the Ghetto to the Main* and *The Jewish Contribution to the Modern World*.

Shandle and Joe King have four granddaughters—Jessica (Mrs. Avi Oppenheimer), Ilana and Joelle Chernack and Erin King.

The Honourable E. Leo Kolber

The Honourable E. Leo Kolber

The Honourable Leo Kolber was Chairman of Claridge Inc., a Montreal-based private management company, until September 1, 1993. For almost 30 years, Leo Kolber was President of CEMP Investments, the business arm of the trusts established by the late Sam Bronfman for his children and grandchildren. During his tenure of office, CEMP concentrated its major efforts on development of real estate in Canada, the United States and Europe.

Leo Kolber is well-known for having established The Fairview Corporation which later became The Cadillac Fairview Corporation, one of the world's leading real estate developers, responsible for landmark buildings such as Toronto's TD Centre, the Eaton Centre and Vancouver's Pacific Centre.

He was a director of The Seagram Company Ltd. from 1971 until 1999; The Toronto-Dominion Bank from 1971 until 1998; and Loews Cineplex Entertainment Corporation from May 1998 to March 2000. He has also served on numerous other boards including E.I. Du Pont Nemours and Company, MGM and Supersol (Israel).

In 1983, he was summoned to the Senate of Canada. He was named Chairman of the Senate Committee on Banking, Trade and Commerce in November 1999, served as a member of the committee from December 1984 until March 1990 and was reinstated in February 1994 until June 2003. On January 18, 2004, he retired from the Senate. He was Chairman of the National Revenue Committee, Liberal Party of Canada.

A lawyer by profession, Leo Kolber was called to the Bar of Quebec in 1952. He received a Doctor of Laws Honoris Causa from Concordia University in 1996 and a Doctor of Laws Honoris Causa from Saint Mary's University in 2001.

He is active in many community, social, cultural and philanthropic activities. In June 1997, he was elected President of the Centre Board of the Sir Mortimer B. Davis - Jewish General Hospital until his resignation in September 1999.

He completed his memoirs, entitled *Leo, a Life*, published by McGill Queen's Press, in October 2003.

Leo Kolber has two children, Lynne Halliday and Jonathan, who now lives in Israel, and four grandchildren.

SHEILA AND MARVYN KUSSNER

Born in Montreal in 1932, Sheila Golden Kussner graduated from McGill University with a Bachelor of Arts degree. She is married to Marvyn Kussner, a Montreal industrialist, and their loving family consists of two daughters, Janice and Joanne, son-in-law John Leopold and grandchildren Justin and Carolyn Leopold.

A health care activist par excellence, Sheila Kussner has earned international recognition as a consummate volunteer and a pioneer in the field of cancer support. In 1981, she founded Hope & Cope, an innovative cancer support program designed to meet the complex emotional and practical needs of cancer patients and their families. Based at the Sir Mortimer B. Davis - Jewish General Hospital, Hope & Cope now comprises 230 compassionate volunteers, and seven highly skilled professional staff who provide program continuity and support.

Since its inception, Hope & Cope has been a model for cancer research centres and hospitals around the world, in countries as far away as Israel and Japan. In recent years, the organization has developed an impressive research stream, with publications in peer-reviewed journals and presentations at international conferences. In fact, Hope & Cope is the only organization of its kind in North America to be engaged in this type of research. As Chairman, Mrs. Kussner remains actively involved in setting the vision and overseeing the day-to-day activities of this unique organization. She continues to raise funds not only for Hope & Cope, but also for the Jewish General Hospital. For example, the hospital's Palliative Care Unit was enhanced and developed through the initiative of Hope & Cope, which also identified a major benefactor to help make this project a reality. Plans are currently underway to establish a Wellness Centre, under the auspices of Hope & Cope, to be located in a home-like setting near the hospital. Once this centre opens, Hope & Cope will truly be able to offer a complete continuum of care at every stage of the cancer experience.

Mrs. Kussner's outstanding contributions to the welfare of cancer patients at the hospital were publicly acknowledged first in 1995, when she received the Jewish General Hospital's Distinguished Service Award, and again in 1999, when the hospital chose to rename Hope & Cope "The Sheila Kussner Hope & Cope Centre".

Sheila Golden Kussner

As a result of her deep and abiding concern for the welfare of cancer patients, Mrs. Kussner played a leadership role in the establishment of the Department of Oncology at McGill University in 1988. She single-handedly raised $25-million for the development of this comprehensive approach to cancer which combines cancer treatment, research and physician training into a unified program within the hospitals of the McGill University network. Thus began a long and productive association with McGill, which appointed her a member of its Board of Governors in 1991. In December, 2004, in recognition of her stellar commitment to the university, she was named a Governor Emeritus.

In addition to the above-mentioned honours, her outstanding contributions to society have earned her numerous prestigious awards and accolades. She is the only Jewish woman in Quebec to be invested as an Officer of the Order of Canada (1995), an Officer of the Order of Quebec (1999) and to have received an honourary Doctorate of Laws from McGill University (1990). Other awards bestowed on her include the Eleanor Roosevelt Humanitarian Award, the President's Medal, conferred by Israel's Head of State, the Medal of Courage from the Canadian Cancer Society, the Samuel Bronfman Medal and the volunteer award for the Montreal region (bénévole remarquable), presented by the Premier of Quebec.

A keynote speaker at Women's Federation's "Choices" event in 1999, Sheila Kussner earned a standing ovation for her riveting account of the choices she made and how her own experience with cancer led her to her life's work as a health care activist. Over the years, she has raised funds for a myriad of organizations including the MSO, Federation CJA and ORT.

MARVYN KUSSNER

A native Montrealer, Marvyn Kussner was born in 1932, and earned a Bachelor of Commerce degree from McGill University. An activist in his own right, he is a well known and respected member of the Montreal Jewish Community. As an entrepreneur, he made his mark in the packaging field, where he served as First President of the Quebec Region's Association of Independent Corrugated Converters. Now retired, he was CEO of Biltwell Containers, a company he led for 50 years.

Marvyn Kussner

Respected for his business acumen, Marvyn Kussner is equally admired for his dedication to the welfare of others and his intimate involvement in community work. He has held many leadership positions over the years, including member of the Board of Directors of the Jewish General Hospital Foundation, Combined Jewish Appeal (Vice-Chairman) and President of the Montefiore Club—an organization with a prestigious roster of members who have achieved a high level of success in the fields of education, health care and government.

Concerned about the lack of information and paucity of research being conducted in the field of prostate cancer in Quebec, in 2002, Mr. Kussner founded and became Chairman of ProCure Alliance, an organization he heads to this day. He immediately set about recruiting Quebec's top business leaders and medical scientists to ProCure's Board of Directors. The mandate of this unique organization is two-fold: to promote education and awareness about prostate cancer, primarily through its comprehensive, fully bilingual website; and to fund avant-garde research through the establishment of a prostate cancer biobank.

Both Marvyn and Sheila Kussner embody the values that Judaism holds dear: charity, faith, and a commitment to making our world a better place. The family enjoys a lifelong membership at Congregation Shaar Hashomayim.

Canada's Jewish Member of Parliament and part-time spy

Canada has had only one Communist Member of Parliament in its existence—and he was the Polish-born Fred Rose, who was the narrow winner in a multi-candidate race in the predominantly Jewish riding of Cartier, in 1943. Rose was a candidate for the Labour-Progressive Party, a thinly-disguised communist group. (Among the other candidates were David Lewis, future leader of the New Democratic Party, and Lazarus Phillips, later a Senator—Paul Martin Sr. labelled him "Canada's greatest parliamentarian"—running for the Liberals. When he was an also-ran, Prime Minister William Lyon MacKenzie King telephoned Phillips to ask "Why did you lose?" "I didn't get enough votes," explained the lawyer.)

The '43 election was an eye-opener for Lewis, whose people checked out a sample of 2,000 listed "voters" and found that 650 were phony. In his book, *Good Fight* (1981), the parliamentarian wrote, "There were names of people who were dead, people who had moved away a year or more before, fictitious addresses."

Rival gangs, going from poll to poll to vote in other people's names, would fight each other with brass knuckles. On occasion, it was found that dogs and cats were registered to vote.

In 1946, a cipher clerk at the Soviet Embassy in Ottawa, Igor Guzenko (who met the press wearing a paper bag over his head) described, in detail, to the Royal Canadian Mounted Police how the Soviets ran a spy ring in Canada, and that Fred Rose was one of their agents! The Member of Parliament was stripped of all privileges (including diplomatic immunity) and sentenced to six years in St. Vincent de Paul Penitentiary (where, if you ask for it, you can have kosher food. The author is aware of only one such request and that was from a convicted murderer, in solitary confinement, who in all likelihood was not Jewish at all. The dozen or so Jewish inmates of the pen generally are incarcerated because of possession and sale of marijuana). Rose was released after five years "for good behaviour" and returned to his native, now-Communist run Poland in 1951. He died there in 1983.

MILDRED LANDE, C.M.

Mildred Lande, C.M., is regarded by many as being the First Lady of the Montreal Jewish Community.

She was the first woman to chair the annual Combined Jewish Appeal (1978)—the community's most awesome responsibility. Previously, she had served as the first President of the Women's Federation, a wing of what was then known as Allied Jewish Community Services (now Federation CJA).

Furthermore, she was the first woman to head up the immense Jewish Community Foundation of Greater Montreal, succeeding the founding chairman, Arthur Pascal. She strengthened the Foundation in a number of imaginative ways, including the formation of its women's division in 1973.

Mrs. Lande was born in Port Arthur, Ontario—the third of five daughters of Abe and Sophie Bronfman.

She graduated from McGill University in 1936, and—a month later—married financier Bernard Lande. He passed away in 1992.

(Mrs. Lande honours her late husband annually with a scholarship to a promising student photographer at Concordia University.)

Mildred and Bernard Lande

Community involvement has been a key element in Mrs. Lande's life, in all its phases.

Her parents were prominent leaders in the development of the Montreal Jewish Community, and her own family, including four children (Neil, Rich, Ruth and Margot) continued the tradition of a strong commitment to community.

"I always worked, even in high school," stated Mrs. Lande in a newspaper interview. "I was always canvassing during campaigns. So, as I raised our four children, I was active."

As a young mother, her first leadership involvement was with the Jewish Junior Welfare League.

She played an important role in organizing the Auxiliary of the Jewish General Hospital, and took over as President in 1960. Under her guidance, Auxiliary membership exploded from 4,000 to more than 10,000. At that time, she noted with justified pride:

"It's the largest women's organization of its kind in Canada."

A unique dimension to Mildred Lande's community role was her utilization of skills in sewing and needlepoint. She taught the creation of designs and needlepoint to other members of the Hospital Auxiliary, earning herself the title of "nimble thimble".

"I always made most of my children's clothes," she once noted.

She served as President of Congregation Shaar Hashomayim, another example of how she pioneered top leadership roles for women—often chairing meetings where men formed the vast majority of participants.

The broad sweep of Milly Lande's achievements has been recognized in a multitude of ways—ranging from the prestigious Order of Canada to an honorary Doctorate of Laws from Concordia University.

Other awards include the Samuel Bronfman Medal—the highest honour of the Canadian Jewish Community, and the Eleanor Roosevelt Centennial Award of Israel Bonds. She was the first Canadian to receive this important recognition. And, at the presentation dinner, the guest speaker was James Roosevelt, son of Eleanor and Franklin Delano Roosevelt.

Mildred Lande is presented with the Order of Canada

In 1986, she was presented with the Endowment Achievement Award of the Council of Jewish Federations, an international organization representing 200 Jewish federations in North America. The text of the award stated that Mrs. Lande was being recognized for "leadership, vision and dedication."

Mrs. Lande has been active, too, in the broader community—playing a leadership role on behalf of the Montreal Museum of Fine Arts, the Montreal Symphony, the Red Cross, the National Ballet of Canada and the campaign against breast cancer.

Mildred Lande resides in an elegant Westmount mansion, only a stone's throw away from her late parents' home. She continues to provide distinguished community leadership, stressing, "Helping other people is a way for me to fulfill myself."

Architect/politician Robert Libman

ROBERT LIBMAN

A native Montrealer, Robert "Bob" Libman switched from architecture to politics when he felt that he could change the direction of Quebec politics—and he did.

Graduating from McGill University in 1985, with a baccalaureat in architecture, he remained at his drafting table (or computer as the technology changed) until 1988. Then, angry over what he regarded as the failure of the Liberal Party to offer little more than a watered down version of the Parti Québécois' ideas for sovereignty, he did the unthinkable—he formed a new political party. In a hectic few months, he and his associates created the Equality Party to represent the interests of those not enamoured of what the Grits and PQ had to offer. He served as leader of the new party from 1988 until 1993, winning the traditionally Liberal D'Arcy McGee seat in 1989. His party won three other seats, setting the political establishment, as it were, "on its ear."

In 1998, he changed direction and ran—unopposed—for the mayor's job in Cote St. Luc, and when the city was merged with Montreal, he became Borough Mayor, and was named to the City of Montreal executive. He served on the Committee responsible for urban planning and development.

On the community side, Bob Libman served as Vice-President of the B'nai Brith Balfour Lodge. And, for a time, he was Executive Director for the fraternal organization in Quebec.

Irving the Barber

When Prince Charles was born, a barber on the Main—doing business as "Irving the Barber"—telexed congratulations to Queen Elizabeth II and Prince Philip. He also offered to provide the Prince with a haircut, without charge, should His Highness happen to need a trim during a visit to Montreal. In their time-honoured tradition, Buckingham Palace responded with a letter on splendid stationery expressing appreciation for his kind words and noting they would keep in mind the offer for a free haircut. Irving thereupon posted the letter in his window and changed his sign to read: "Irving—Barber to the Royal Family."

Frederick Lowy

Professor Frederick Lowy, President Emeritus of Montreal's Concordia University, was born in Grosspetersdorf, Austria, on January 1, 1933—30 days before Adolf Hitler came to power in neighbouring Germany.

He and his family left Austria, then incorporated into the Reich, in September 1938, and reached Montreal in 1945, when Dr. Lowy was 12.

He studied at McGill University, graduating with a B.A. in 1955, and an MD, CM in 1959. After postgraduate training in internal medicine and psychiatry in Montreal and Cincinnati, he returned to McGill and the Royal Victoria Hospital as a psychiatric consultant. Subsequent psychiatric posts included department head at the Ottawa Civic Hospital and Toronto's Clarke Institute of Psychiatry, of which he was director. At the same time, he was Professor and Chairman of the University of Toronto Department of Psychiatry. He went on to become Dean of Medicine, and founder of the Centre for Bioethics at the University of Toronto.

In 1995, he returned to Montreal to become Rector, and later, President of Concordia, for a 10-year span.

Dr. Lowy is a highly respected medical educator. He is a Fellow of the Royal College of Physicians and Surgeons, a Life Member of both the Canadian and American Psychiatric Associations, and of the American College of Psychiatrists.

He was named an Officer of the Order of Canada in 2000.

Dr. Lowy is married to Dr. Mary Kay O'Neill Lowy and they have four children, and four granddaughters

The Honourable Mr. Justice Herbert Marx

Mr. Justice Marx was born in Montreal on March 16, 1932.

There were great things expected from Herbert Marx when he placed first in the Quebec Bar Exams, in 1968. His winning of the Prix du Barreau de Paris did, indeed, indicate that he was bound for a remarkable career.

Mr. Justice Herbert Marx

That career has taken him from the classroom, as a professor of Constitutional Law, to the Quebec National Assembly, to the Cabinet as Minister of Justice and Attorney General, and most recently, to the Bench as a Justice of the Quebec Superior Court.

Justice Marx studied at Concordia University (Bachelor of Arts, 1958), Université de Montréal (Master of Arts, 1962, and Law degree, 1967) and, finally, Harvard Law School (Master of Laws Degrees, 1969).

He was awarded Canada Council and Quebec Government Scholarships in 1968 and 1969.

He worked in the business world, as Vice-President of an electrical lighting company, for 10 years (1954-1964) before taking his skills into the classroom at the Université de Montréal as a Professor of Constitutional Law, 1969-1979.

From 1975-1979, he was Commissioner of the Quebec Human Rights Commission, as well as a member of the Advisory Council, Institute of Governmental Affairs, Queen's University.

In 1979, he ran for and was elected the Liberal member of the Quebec National Assembly for D'Arcy McGee. He remained a member of the Assembly for a decade, joining the cabinet for three years. He stepped down when he disagreed with government policy.

In 1989, he was named to the Bench.

Justice Marx has published books and many articles on constitutional law, law and poverty, and civil liberties.

Over the years, Justice Marx has been involved in the work of many community organizations. He is now co-chair of the McGill Middle East Program in Civil Society and Peace Building; Honorary Governor, Jewish General Hospital; Governor, Canadian Friends of Tel Aviv University; active in Canadian Jewish Congress (Quebec Region).

He is married to Eva Felsenburg. They have two children, Robert and Sarah, and three grandchildren.

"It is the supreme art of the teacher to awaken joy in creative expression and knowledge."

Albert Einstein,
speaking at Pasadena Junior College

Greta Matus

"My roots in Montreal go back to the 19th Century, when my mother, Sarah Segal, was born in 1895, the eldest of eight children born to Meyer and Jennie Segal. She married my father, Jacob Blanshay, who came to Montreal as a child, with his family, from Russia.

I attended Strathcona Academy and McGill University, where I graduated with a Bachelor of Arts degree and a high school teaching diploma.

Although my first cousins Herschel Segal of Le Chateau and Alvin Segal of Peerless Clothing are prominent in the business world, I chose teaching as my profession.

(Peerless Clothing was created and developed by my mother's brothers, Moe and Phil Segal.

Greta Matus taught mathematics to more than 3,000 students, over 30 years, at Herzliah High School.

I taught mathematics at Herzliah High School for many years, and was appointed head of the Mathematics Department when that position was introduced in the school.

When I first began to teach, Irving Layton, an icon of Canadian literature, was a colleague.

During my early years as a teacher, I could not believe that I was getting paid do to what I loved. The students were so eager to learn, and I was so anxious to teach and give them the benefit of my knowledge.

I demanded much from my students, as I wanted them to achieve as high a standard as they were capable of. As teenagers, they sometimes objected to what I asked of them, but with maturity they realized that my requirements made sense and that they benefited from them.

On Rosh Hashanah, meeting a former student at synagogue, I was pleasantly surprised when he told me that at a recent 20-year reunion of his class, 25 students of his class had voted me the teacher who had the most positive influence on their lives.

I have fond memories of many prominent people who were former students of mine, in a wide variety of professions and positions, from Irwin Cotler, Minister of Justice and Attorney General of Canada; Hugh Segal, one-time advisor to Prime Minister Brian Mulroney (and now a Senator); Robert Libman, Borough Mayor of Cote St. Luc; Charles Krauthammer, a free-lance journalist who writes for *Time* magazine and *The Economist*.

There are many physicians, dentists, lawyers, accountants, etc., both in Montreal, Toronto, the rest of Canada, and the U.S.A., who were my students, too numerous to mention. However, to mention a few, there is Gerald Batist, head of the Cancer Centre at the Jewish General Hospital; Dr. Mitchell Shulman, who was heard regularly on radio station CJAD providing medical advice.

Also there was Deborah Cohen, an obstetrician; Carol Ann Vasilfsky, a gastroenterologist; Mark Sherman, an endocrinologist, and an assistant professor at McGill University. In addition, there is Joseph Gauze, an otorhinolaryngologist; Mitchell Rubinowitz, an orthopedic surgeon; Mark Hoffman, an oncologist and Michael Segal, a neurosurgeon.

I taught about 3,000 students in my career. The variety of life careers among them is quite unusual. Morty Yalofsky is Dean of McGill University. Moses Znaimer is the owner and director of the Bravo television broadcasting system, based in Toronto. Stephen Schipper is the director of the Manitoba Theatre Centre in Winnipeg. Stephen Schecter is a professor at Université du Québec à Montréal (UQAM); Harold Lieberman is a dentist. Syvia Ryback Sklar is Associate Director at the Centre for Leadership, at McGill University's Department of Education. Howard Busgang is a successful comedian. Brenda Bessner is a financial reporter, appearing regularly on the CTV network. Melvin Segal is a psychologist who is mentioned in Margaret Trudeau's book about her visit, with her children, to him.

In addition to the customary careers of bright students, those who graduated from a Jewish religious school, such as Herzliah, followed many different paths.

I married Victor Matus, a successful entrepreneur in plastics, who gave me the choice to leave teaching to pursue other interests. We have two children, Jeffrey and Rachelle, who both graduated from McGill.

During my years of teaching, my husband and I travelled to many countries during summer vacations. After I left teaching, we continued to travel, visiting Israel, Eastern and Western Europe, England, France, Italy, Switzerland, Holland, Belgium, Liechtenstein, Luxembourg, Czechoslovakia, Hungary and many parts of Canada and the United States. We visited East Berlin when it was in the Russian zone, namely so we could see the Great Synagogue which was the first casualty of the Kristallnacht.

Then in 2003, we revisited the same synagogue which was rebuilt to its former splendour.

When I decided to leave teaching, in order to follow other interests, I became involved with Women's Federation of CJA. I was and am a canvasser for many years. I was also actively involved in running French courses, which Women's Federation sponsored with the support of the Quebec Government.

I was part of McGill Learning in Retirement from its inception. I also participated regularly at the YM-YWHA.

My husband and I financially support many Jewish organizations on a regular basis. My husband gave a substantial donation to the Jewish Community Foundation to establish a fund in his name. He is also an active supporter of our synagogue. We are both deeply committed to the welfare of Israel and we purchase Israel Bonds regularly.

I am a Life Member of Hadassah, a member of Emunah Women, Jewish Women International, and the Jewish General Hospital Auxiliary. I support some yeshivas because I believe that the study of our religious texts is the basis of our survival as a nation.

The Man They Called "Moses"

Among the many skilled Jewish immigrants who arrived in Montreal in the early years of the 20th Century was a carpenter named Thomas Batshaw, who planned to stay one night with a cousin before continuing on to New York. However, over dinner, Batshaw learned that the Canadian Pacific Railway in Montreal was hiring skilled tradesmen. He walked down to the rail yards (the street car ride cost 7 cents!) the next morning to try his luck. He never made it to New York. Thomas was hired and worked for more than 30 years for the railway. Along the way, he and his wife had three children—including Harry Batshaw, Canada's first Jewish judge and Manuel G. Batshaw, a much-honoured social worker. When it came time to retire, Thomas was not strong enough to lug his heavy box of tools—so he sent his son Manny to pick them up. "I've come for Thomas Batshaw's toolbox, Manny said to the shop supervisor. The official looked puzzled, "I've never heard of a Thomas Batshaw." Then he turned to workmen standing nearby. "Any of you ever heard of a Thomas Batshaw?" he asked. Unanimously, they indicated they had never heard of anyone with that name. An astonished Manuel G. responded, "But he has worked here for more than 30 years!" Then one of the workers piped up—"He must mean 'Moses'." On the company payroll, Thomas Batshaw was so listed, but to his fellow workers, he was Moses!

Dorothy Reitman, C.M.

Community volunteer and activist locally, nationally and internationally, Mrs. Reitman's major concerns include Human Rights, Status of Women, Poverty, Family, Elderly and Environment.

She was the first female President of Canadian Jewish Congress (1986-1989).

Mrs. Reitman's past activities include President, National Council of Jewish Women of Canada, President Canadian Jewish Congress and Chair of the North American Committee of the International Council of Jewish Women.

She has served as an officer of Women's Federation of Allied Jewish Community Services (now known as Federation CJA), La Federation des Femmes du Québec and the Montreal Council of Women.

As a board member, Mrs. Reitman's involvement included the Canadian Association of Ben Gurion University, Golden Age Association of Montreal, Allied Jewish Community Services of Montreal, Canadian Mental Health Association, La Santé Mentale de Québec, Match International Centre, Neighbourhood House and the Auberge Shalom for Battered Women (founding member).

Mrs. Reitman's fundraising activities have included Associate Chair, Combined Jewish Appeal, Women's Division; Federated Appeal of Greater Montreal (Centraide); Canadian Cancer Society Special Names.

She is currently Chair of the Canada Committee of the Commonwealth Jewish Council; Co-chair of the International Council of Jewish Women (ICJW); Women in Enterprise and Profession (WEP) Networking Project, and Honourary Chair of the Friends Committee of the McGill University Centre for Research and Teaching on Women.

She is presently an active board member of the Cummings House Centre for Senior Citizens; Mazon Canada; the Canadian Council of Christians and Jews; Chances Foundation, and the Portage Program for Drug Dependency (founding member).

Community Awards include:

Member of the Order of Canada (1987)
Queen's Jubilee Medal (1967)
Queen's Golden Jubilee Medal (2002)
Governor General's Award in Commemoration of Persons Case (1992)

Montreal Jewish Community Leadership Award (1965)
Commonwealth Jewish Council Award (1989)
B'nai Brith (Women) Toronto Woman of the Year (1986)
Women's League of Conservative Judaism (1986)

Dorothy is married to Cyril Reitman and they have one son, Joel, and two grandsons, Sam and Richard.

The Rubenstein Family

Louis Rubenstein

Louis Rubenstein was a remarkable Montrealer—sportsman, industrialist and politician.

Born in Montreal in 1861, he went on to become the first amateur figure skating champion of the world (1890), was known as the father of figure skating (he apparently introduced figure skating into Canada), and the father, too, of bowling. He served as a city alderman for a remarkable 17 years (from 1914 until his death in 1931). He had seven brothers (Israel, Abraham, Lazarus, Isaac, Moses, Jacob and Barnet), and four sisters, (Sarah, Jenny, Rachel and Florence or Fanny).

Louis was an international sports figure.

His parents, Leah and Max, were immigrants from Poland (1850), and among the pioneer 40 Jewish families who settled in Montreal. Max had been Burgomaster of his town. A learned Hebrew scholar, he joined the Spanish and Portuguese Congregation shortly after his arrival. He and members of his family were to be prominent in the affairs of the synagogue for years.

Leah Rubenstein

Leah Rubenstein gave birth to 12 children between 1839 and 1865—a span of 26 years! When Max and Leah came to Montreal in 1850, they brought four children with them. Apparently she had been married at 16 or 17. And she was only in her 50s when she died in 1876. The Board of Trustees of the Spanish and Portuguese Synagogue, in a tribute, referred to her sterling qualities and virtues.

For a time, Max and Leah and their entire family, a total of 13 people (except Florence who had moved to Fort Wayne) lived above their shop at 537 1/2 Craig Street.

St. Petersburg, in Imperial Russia, in 1890—virtually the world capital of anti-Semitism.

Strangely enough, only four of the Rubensteins married, and only two of them had children. One married a non-Jewish woman, and Florence (who married a Cohen) moved away from Montreal.

While all members of the family were respected and important members of the community, Louis was the towering figure—honoured in North America and, ultimately, on the international level.

After Louis won the figure skating championships of Canada and the United States (1885), friends collected a handsome purse of $400 to send him to St. Petersburg, Russia, for the first World Amateur figure skating title. No one seemed to appreciate the fact that at that time, 1890, the Imperial Russian leader, Czar Alexander, was a fierce anti-Semite.

Louis Rubenstein, wearing the winner's ribbon, at the St. Petersburg competition.

The Secret Service seizes Louis

When the 28-year-old Louis arrived in St. Petersburg, he was detained by members of the Russian Secret Service, and ordered to leave. Fortunately, the Montreal skater had a very influential friend back in Canada—the Governor General, Lord Stanley (the National Hockey League's Stanley Cup honours his name). Lord Stanley had given the athlete a letter calling on British diplomats (Canada had no international representation at this time) to assist him and the English ambassador, Sir Robert Morier, arranged for him to be freed. Sir Robert declared: "A British subject who comes to Russia to take part in an international match, will be allowed to stay, and you will stay until you compete."

Lord Stanley was a fan. The year before Rubenstein's triumph in St. Petersburg, the Ottawa Free Press reported: "Mr. Louis Rubenstein, the celebrated fancy skater of Montreal, had luncheon at Rideau Hall yesterday, by invitation, after which he gave a fancy skating exhibition in the curling rink before Lord and Lady Stanley, Madame Albani, Sir James Grant, Sir George Baden-Powell and others.

The skill of the skater delighted the vice-regal party and the visitors."

Louis goes for a spin in 1917 with the Mayor of Kingston, Ontario.

Even then, in this terrible atmosphere, it would seem unlikely—to say the least—that Louis Rubenstein would have a chance of winning the title. The judges, it was reported, were prejudiced. But he was such an immensely talented skater that, when all the competitors had performed, there was no question who had won. And the Czar—who had driven Jews out of his country, forced them to convert or impoverished them—was compelled to honour the Montrealer.

And Louis Rubenstein was greeted as a celebrity as he journeyed home to Canada—hosted by royalty in both Berlin (by the Kaiser himself) and London, where he was escorted by the Prince of Wales, later King Edward VII. He was welcomed home to Montreal by cheering crowds at Bonaventure station, when he stepped down from the Central Vermont train.

The headline of one Montreal newspaper read: "Well Done! Rubenstein."

Then, aged 28, he announced he was retiring from competition to open the way for some "young fellar" to compete.

Alderman Louis Rubenstein

Louis was active in the family business—Rubenstein Brothers metal platers and manufacturers, but he continued to devote a great deal of time to sports.

The family had wide interests

Obviously Louis and his brothers and sisters were more than outstanding athletes. They also were leaders in the formation and functioning of key sports groups.

Louis was President of the Amateur Skating Association; President of the Montreal Amateur Athletic Association (1913-1915) ; President and Life Governor of the Royal Life Saving Society, Quebec Branch; President of the

Skating with a sister (Sarah or Rachel)

St. Andrew's Curling Club; Vice-President of the Canadian Bowling League; President and Honorary President (for 18 years!) of the Canadian Wheelman's Association; President of the International Skating Union of America and, finally, President of the Young Men's Hebrew Association, for 12 years, beginning in 1916.

In 1885, Lazarus and Louis convened a meeting at the popular Hope Coffee House and this led to the formation of the Canadian Amateur Skating Association.

Louis Rubenstein took to civic politics readily, feeling that an elected position would help strengthen his community work.

He first threw his hat into the aldermanic ring in 1912, in the St. Louis ward. He won without opposition and he was re-elected, unopposed, in every election until his death other than the final electoral contest.

He refused to accept any remuneration, turning everything he earned in political life to charities.

Occasionally, he served as acting mayor, greeting important visitors to the city.

A drinking fountain in Fletcher's Field (at the corner of Mount Royal and Park Avenues) bears his name and, until 2004, was the only monument honouring a Jew in the city. (The city named a park in honour of Hirsch Wolofsky, founder of the Yiddish daily, *The Kanader Adler*, in 2004.)

His funeral was one of the largest ever seen in Montreal and among those paying tribute to him was Mayor Camilien Houde. As was the custom then, it took place from his home, 3567 St. Urbain Street.

Twelve mounted policemen served as an advance guard for the funeral procession, and a further 150 police officers emphasized the importance of Louis Rubenstein to Montrealers.

One speaker at the funeral said of him: "He was kindly, tolerant, friendly and charitable, qualities which endeared him to all classes and creeds of men."

Rabbi Charles Bender, conducting the services at the Spanish and Portuguese Synagogue, told the crowded hall that "Louis Rubenstein is mourned as a perfect combination of a fine Canadian and a Jew."

The Montreal *Gazette*, in his obituary, declared "in the death of Ald. Rubenstein there has passed a good citizen who figured prominently in business, social, public and sports life for nearly half a century."

The Montreal Star added that he "brought fame to his city and to the Dominion."

Seven brothers and four sisters

Other Rubenstein siblings also were prominent and respected, and were outstanding amateur sports people. Israel (1848-1930) was director of the Agriculture Society and also helped many immigrants to settle in Canada. Furthermore, he was treasurer of the Montreal Choral Society.

Abraham (1853-1922) was a strong supporter of community organizations, particularly the Talmud Torahs. In 1904, he won the Earl Grey Prize in figure skating for beginners. He may have encouraged Louis in his skating career.

Lazarus (1855- 1930) was active in the Y.M.H.A. and in Scottish Curling Circles. He became known as "The Professor of Curling." And in track and field, he won the 120-yard hurdle championship and sprinted 100 yards in 10 seconds flat.

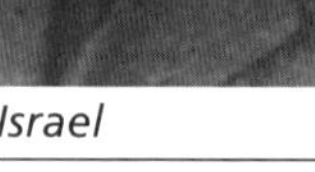

Israel

Abraham

Lazarus

Barnet

Sarah

Jacob (1839-1930) lived to be 91 and served, for a time, on the Union side of the American Civil War.

Isaac (1854-1877) and Barnet (1846-1921) were widely active in the Jewish community but focused mostly on synagogues and Talmud Torahs. Barnet was an original partner in the family business but later went into footwear and moved to Michigan.

Members of the Rubenstein family relax in their garden.

Israel (1848-1930) was 20 when he attended his first synagogue meeting and in 1897, he was named to the most prestigious post of the congregation, Parnass. He held that position of honour for a remarkable 52 years! He was the treasurer when the first Zionist organization was set up in Montreal. And he was one of seven members of the Canadian Zionists Council. He was among the founders of the Young Men's Hebrew Benevolent Society. And he was one of the group involved in contacting the Baron de Hirsch and arranging for the gift (of $20,000) launching the Baron de Hirsch Institute.

Sarah (1859-1929) was President for six years of the Ladies Hebrew Benevolent Society. In 1901, she won the American Ladies Skating Championship. She was described as an "excellent coloratura soprano," and she and her sisters held recitals and bazaars to raise money for assistance programs for immigrants.

Florence or Fanny (1847-1911) was also well-known as a singer, and contributed her talents to many charitable fund-raising activities.

Jenny (1862-1890) joined members of the family in working on both Jewish and general charities in the city.

Rachel (1863-1937) won the American Ladies skating championship. Apparently, at 19, she also became involved in the family business as a silver plater.

Moses (1865-1929) won the Canadian figure skating championship in 1904.

RUBENSTEIN,
RUBENSTEIN!!
FRIDAY EVENING, MARCH 14TH. 1884,
AT THE
MIRAMICHI SKATING & CURLING RINK, NEWCASTLE.
MR. LOUIS RUBENSTEIN,
THE Champion FANCY SKATER OF America!!

The Directors of the Rink have much pleasure in announcing that Mr. RUBENSTEIN has consented to remain over at Newcastle on his return to Montreal, and give an exhibition of his magnificent Fancy Skating.

RACES! WILL BE HELD AS FOLLOWS:-
5 Mile Race, free for all. 1 Mile Race, boys of 15 and under.

A first prize of a handsome Silver Cup will be awarded to the winner of the 5 mile race, with second and third cash prizes of $3 and $2. Cash prizes of $3 and $2 will be given the winners of the one mile race.
There must be five entries in each competition.

THE RINK BRASS BAND WILL BE IN ATTENDANCE
The Event of the Season!
Admission 25 cents. Children 15 cents. Entries to Races, 25 cents.
TICKETS AT THE DRUG STORES
CHAS. SARGEANT, President. JOHN FERGUSON, Sec'y Treas.

The Rubensteins as industrialists

Max Rubenstein earned a living working, initially, as a glazier. Fourteen years after his arrival in Canada, he organized

Rubenstein Brothers Silver Platers—in 1864—three years before Confederation. They were silver, gold and nickel platers, and manufacturers. The brothers started with a brass foundry, more than 140 years ago, eventually plating silver, gold and nickel and expanding into manufacturing.

In 1929, Louis Rosenblum, as the last surviving partner, sold the company to Jack and Dave Becker.

The company thrives today, but is very much aware of the debt owed to the Rubenstein family.

JUDGE BARBARA SEAL, C.M.

Donald and Barbara Seal

Barbara Seal was appointed a Citizenship Judge in 1997 and has had her mandate continuously renewed. She serves in this capacity across Canada and particularly in Montreal.

Mrs. Seal enjoys a distinguished career in public and community service. She was a Municipal Councillor in Hampstead from 1980 to 2001, and volunteers her services to countless charitable, civic and cultural organizations.

As councillor, she had specific responsibilities for parks, playgrounds and recreational activities, and was instrumental in developing the town's Neighbourhood Watch and Crime Prevention programs.

She served as Editor of the *Hampstead Journal*, as Chairperson of the Hampstead Winter Carnival, as Chairperson of the town's 75th Anniversary Celebrations, and was responsible for all the town's holiday and civic celebrations.

Mrs. Seal acted as Chairperson of the Canadian Cancer Society; Director of the Canadian Twinning Association, Vice-President of Canada Day Celebrations in Quebec, Chairperson of the jury judging Canada Day Posters and Chairperson of Canada Day Youth Awards. She has served on the Board of Directors of Place des Arts, on the Arts Council of the Montreal Urban community, on the Board of Directors of the Children's Wish Foundation and is a member on the National Forum on Climate Change.

Mrs. Seal is an active supporter of Tel Aviv University where she is a member of the Board of Governors and National President of its Canadian Friends. She recently was honoured by the University and received its prestigious President's Medal.

Mrs. Seal has been honoured by many organizations for her commitment to community service, receiving the Golda Meir Award from the State of Israel Bonds Organization, the Jerusalem 3000 Medal, awards from the Canadian Parks and Recreation Association and the Canadian Cancer Society. She is a recipient of both the Commemorative Medal for the 125th Anniversary of Canadian Confederation and the Special Edition Plaque presented by the Governor General as one of 125 volunteers from across Canada who made an outstanding contribution. She is a recipient of the Queen's Golden Jubilee Commemorative Medal.

Mrs. Seal is a member of the Committee to promote events for the Montreal Chamber Orchestra and is on the Organizing Committee of the McGill Middle East Peace Program. She was honoured with a medal from the Carrefour des Communautés du Québec.

Her services to the community were recognized by the Government of Canada who bestowed upon her the Order of Canada.

Donald W. Seal, Q.C.

Donald W. Seal, Q.C., is an active practising attorney and senior partner in the firm Seal Seidman, s.e.n.c. He specializes in corporate and commercial matters and has pleaded before most courts and tribunals in Canada and has established important juridical principles in the Supreme Court.

He is a retired Municipal Court Judge having presided for 15 years in courts about the province of Quebec, sitting principally in Hampstead, Cote Saint-Luc, Chateauguay, Delson, Saint Constant and Dollard-des-Ormeaux.

He is active in charitable and communal work, acting in many instances as legal counsel. He devotes much time to the Canadian Friends of Tel Aviv University, where he is a member of the Board of Directors.

Mr. Seal is also active in commercial enterprises and sits on various Boards of Directors. He was Chairman of the Board of Sportscene Restaurants Inc. in 1993 and 1994.

He graduated from McGill University with a BCL in 1954, was received at the Bar in 1955, and was named a Queen's Counsel in 1974.

DR. HARVEY HAROLD SIGMAN

Harvey Sigman has combined an outstanding career as a surgeon with a variety of leadership roles in the Montreal Jewish Community.

He served as President of Federation CJA (formerly Allied Jewish Community Services) 1981-1983, headed up the Jewish Cultural Association 1985-1996 and was Founding President of Jewish Support Services for the Elderly, 1988-1991.

He is a graduate in Medicine from McGill University, a Professor of Surgery at McGill University and was Chief of the Division of General Surgery at the Jewish General Hospital.

Dr. Sigman is a Fellow of the Royal College of Physicians and Surgeons of Canada and of the American College of Surgeons.

He has had a major interest in Medical Education and has played a role in curriculum development at a local and international level. He served as Assistant Dean, Medical Education and Student Affairs, in the Faculty of Medicine, McGill University, 1993-1997.

He has been the recipient of the Canadian Forces Decoration (1985) Governor General's Medal (Queens Jubilee 1977), the Samuel Bronfman Medal (Canadian Jewry's highest honour) 1991 and teaching awards.

He is a retired Lieutenant-Colonel in the Royal Canadian Army Medical Corps.

Dr. Sigman is married to Maxine (Strean) and they have four children—Eric Henry, Terry Ellen (Zlotnick) and Karen Gay (Laxer).

DR. MAXINE STREAN SIGMAN

Dr. Maxine Sigman is a clinical psychologist who has been in private practice since 1981. She is, as well, the staff psychologist on the in-patient psychiatry service at the Sir Mortimer B. Davis Jewish General Hospital. She is an Assistant Professor in the Department of Psychiatry at McGill University.

Her involvement in community is not surprising. Her late father, Dr. George Strean, was a prominent community leader.

Dr. Sigman has played a number of leadership roles—serving as President of Federation CJA, (formerly Allied Jewish Community Services) 1989-1991. Prior to that, she had undertaken increasingly heavy community responsibilities—going from Chairman of the Women's Division of the Combined Jewish Appeal in 1972 to heading up the Federation's Planning and Allocations Committee, from 1983-1985; and then serving as Chairman of the Federation's Executive Committee.

Following her presidency of the Federation, Dr. Sigman chaired the Council on Services to Families and Children for several years and then spearheaded a Council on Services for individuals with Special Needs.

Maxine Sigman's leadership qualities were recognized very early. In 1968, she was awarded the Barkoff Leadership Award. In 1999, Dr. Sigman was awarded the Samuel Bronfman Medal for distinguished community service.

She is married to Dr. Harvey Sigman and their three children are all physicians practising in Montreal. They enjoy eight grandsons.

Allan Bronfman and the Humourist

No one questions that Stephen Leacock was Canada's greatest humourist. Some of the greatest in the field, including Bob Benchley of New York and Hollywood, acknowledged their debt to Leacock—famous for trotting across the McGill University campus, in winter-time, wearing a moth-eaten fur coat, always open whatever the temperature. While the McGill academic had an extraordinary sense of humour, he still absorbed many of the prejudices of the first half of the 20th Century. So when Sam Bronfman asked Leacock to write a history of Canada to strengthen Canadian morale during the dark, early days of World War II, he was wandering into a minefield. "I need a place to work," Leacock stated right away. And Sam's younger brother, Allan, said, "You can use my study." (Allan and Sam lived back to back on the slopes of Mount Royal, in Westmount, sharing only a swimming pool.) However, when the history was completed, Mr. Sam was alarmed to find it was filled with a variety of sharp criticism, ranging from snide remarks about French Canadians and the Roman Catholic Church, to stinging comment on the United States, the Irish, people who had large fortunes, and statements indicating a total lack of understanding of the contribution immigrants, including those from Eastern Europe, had made to the nation. Negotiating compromises on the text were beyond Mr. Sam so he brought in his speechwriter, the famed poet/lawyer A.M. Klein , who acted as an intermediary. The final result was *Canada: The Foundations of its Future,* which still shows up in used book stores and which continues to be used by the Bronfman family, in a limited edition form with a slipcase, as a gift to Very Important People. (Recipients have included Joseph Stalin, Dictator of the Soviet Union, and comedian Jack Benny!) When the exercise was completed, Allan Bronfman donated his study, with its magnificent wood panelling, to McGill University where, today, it is the Leacock Room of the University's Rare Book Division—filled with the works of Leacock, paintings of the humourist, etc.

Heather Solomon

CJN arts columnist Heather Solomon

(Long-time *Canadian Jewish News* arts columnist on her coverage of the performing and visual arts for the past 26 years)

I have always had two loves, art and the theatre. A Concordia University joint major, in theatre arts and visual arts, allowed me to indulge them both. My theatre professor, Norma Springford, enjoyed a class assignment play review I'd written, and told me to march up to *The Georgian* on the 6th floor and announce myself as their new theatre critic. But the student newspaper was desperate for a political cartoonist, so until Dave Haney showed up, whose sole aim was to cartoon, that's what I was doing. At that time, the CEGEPS were in the universities, so I spent the two years of junior college, plus the three years of my Bachelor of Fine Arts with Distinction, and a year of advanced studies, at the paper as theatre critic and entertainment editor.

Upon graduation, a series of jobs at short-lived dailies (like *The Montreal Record*), award-winning magazine work and infrequent free-lancing for *The Gazette* prompted a friend, playwright Carol Libman, to tell me about an opening at *The Canadian Jewish News*. There, she pointed out, I could develop an ongoing forum for my arts commentary. That was in 1979. Soon, the column posted a photo of me with my by-line. The photo changed four times over the next 26 years, evolving with the style of my eyeglasses! I've critiqued and interviewed every week since that first column, except for the two weeks we don't publish, one in July, the other in December. I even wrote my column while I was in the throes of labour with my first child. That's 1,300 columns, so far, a multiple of the b'nai mitzvah coming of age and, in excess of that number, the many times that the Toronto and Internet editions have picked up my columns.

In our Montreal microcosm, I have never been at a loss for a story. As certain subjects' work evolved over the years, I'd write another article on them but more often, I found new artists. In the field of art, some of my memorable interviews have been with Louis Muhlstock (as this artist continued to produce well into his 90s), Ghitta Caiserman-Roth, Rita Briansky, Paul Lancz, Stanley Lewis, Eric Wesselow, Sylvia Safdie, Seymour Segal, Melvin Charney (the CCA sculpture garden), Marcel Braitstein, Yehouda Chaki, Peter Krausz, Marion Wagschal, Morton Rosengarten,

Stephen Lack, Roslyn Swartzman, Leopold Plotek, David Feist, to name only a few. The tapes and transcripts from many of these artists, some now deceased, are valuable to me as nuggets from their lives. I will likely conceive of a book project in the future.

My interview style is to ask about someone's earliest recollections of creativity and follow it through their lives. Inevitably a thread of development binds one stage to another, with respect to their output.

Having a Jewish focus for my work enfolds me in the community. The sense of family is overwhelming—these are my people and I am theirs, and it's this that somehow gives me the license to ask personal questions and query them more deeply about their creative process than would other journalists. Then, after I've transcribed and meditated on the material, and I've taken notes of my gut impressions of their art or performance, I go, in my mind, to what I call "another place" where I channel their emotions and mine into prose.

I don't see my allowance of 650 to 800 words as a limitation but rather as a challenge in which to express the essence of my subject. Every word counts. I'm gratified to receive letters from my subjects who know it's been more than a journalistic exercise for me. Harry Mayerovitch wrote to me on June 19, 2000: "I was particularly impressed with the particularity of your approach. Not a superficial overall view, but an immersing in the individual works and their implication. I am once again appreciative of your sensitivity..." In 1997, David Feist penned, "Not only do you have a good eye, you even listen — an unfortunately rare quality." Really listening to what an artist is telling me, seeing past the paint or the stone and into the heart of the work, these are my ultimate goals.

There are the artists from "away" that I have had the opportunity to interview, like celebrated photographer Annie Leibovitz, Israeli painter Ivan Schwebel, Steve Kaufman, Leon Golub, George Segal. Often, people ask me, "So who have you interviewed that's famous?" I can drop these names but I'll tell you that our Montreal Jewish artists are every bit as deserving.

In the realm of the theatre, I've interviewed the likes of Maurice Podbrey, Muriel Gold, Dora Wasserman, Dorothy Davis Stein who ran the Montreal Children's Theatre for more than 50 years, Sam Gesser, Alexander Hausvater, Howard Ryshpan, Seymour Blicker, Aviva Ravel. In from Toronto were Al Waxman and Sylvia Lennick ("I told him, 'Julie, don't go!'") and, from "away," Melville Shavelson, Oded Teomi, Peter Frye, Arnold Wesker, Paul Hecht.

In film/TV, there's been Donald Winkler, Robert Lantos, Felix Lazarus, Harold Greenberg, George Bloomfield, James Shavick, Ted Allan, Harry Gulkin, Saul Rubinek and from away , Fyvush Finkel, Ron Perlman, Jane Seymour.

In dance, I've spoken with Edouard Lock, Ohad Naharin and others.

Music, the Brott family, of course: Alexander and his sons Boris and Denis; Yuli Turovsky, the late great saxophonist Gerald Danovitch and conductors Uri Mayer and Yoav Talmi. Pop music has included Neil Sedaka.

Literature: Isaac Bashevis Singer, Martin Gray, William Weintraub and the list goes on. That all of these creative souls are Jewish is, to my mind, no coincidence. Judaism fosters an awareness of the seen and the unseen, a certain penchant for self-expression. The Jewish urge to question and examine is ingrained, to follow paths of curiosity, to define life in ways that transcend methodical analysis. The Jewish way, even if the artist is not religious, is a spiritual way, connecting to the Almighty along nerve paths of which we aren't even consciously aware. It is my privilege to have had my column as the best excuse in the world to approach these creators and funnel their gifts into my words.

Norm Spector

Norm Spector has had a varied career—ranging from rescuing Holocaust-ravaged Jews in 1945 Germany, to providing national leadership to Israel Bonds, to demonstrating expertise on fuel and energy conservation.

Norm Spector—a 19-year-old soldier in the U.S. Army

Norm was born in New York, in 1926, and was taken to Montreal at age 4.

As a youth, he shared back-breaking work with his father who ran a coal delivery business. Norm became muscled and wiry from hefting 200-pound bags of coal.

While studying at Baron Byng High School, he alternated studies with the challenge of keeping three part-time jobs.

In 1945, seeking adventure, he joined the United States Army. As a persistent over-achiever, Norm became the youngest basic training instructor ever at Fort Dix, New Jersey. He was sent overseas to join the American occupation forces in Europe. There he was shocked when he encountered starved, emaciated concentration camp survivors.

Deeply moved, he worked with the United Nations Refugee Organization, focusing on helping thousands of homeless and hungry Jews.

In time, he became a liaison between the U.S. Army and the American Joint Distribution Committee, the Jewish group working with refugees.

On one occasion, he remembers, "I led three trainloads of 1,200 displaced persons from Germany into France and Marseilles." From the French Mediterranean port, they were able to get to Palestine.

He returned to Montreal in 1948 and, once more, while attending McGill University, he was back at work with his father. "We carried 200-pound bags of coal 18 hours a day to customers bigger companies didn't want to service."

The heating business changed drastically in 1949 when oil become popular. Norm borrowed $5,000, bought an oil truck—and modernized the family business "That truck went with me wherever I went; I parked it on the campus between classes, working seven days a week." Mordecai Richler, in *St. Urbain's Horseman*, mentions Norm and his oil truck but doesn't identify him.

A different aspect of his life: trained as a life guard in the U.S. Army, he has saved seven people from drowning!

Norm was deeply immersed in his growing business—but in 1968, his world turned upside down when he was persuaded to join a Study Mission to Israel.

Norm Spector with his close friend Edward Bronfman—working partners for the Jewish community.

After that, the Jewish community shared his life with his family (wife Selma, two sons and a daughter) and his business.

In 1975, he accepted the heaviest community responsibility of them all: he served as General Chairman of the Montreal Combined Jewish Appeal.

Two years later, he began a long involvement with Israel Bonds.

Norm Spector became an expert on fuel and energy conservation, writing two books, *Man and His Home* and *Save Money—Save Energy*.

He invented a heating system using garbage, wood, coal... virtually any combustible and installed it in the home of Marcel Einhorn.

He invented an electric car which was shown at a Detroit auto show where it won First Prize. Oddly enough, in Montreal, it won only second prize!

In the heating field, Norm Spector steadily moved up the ladder, joining S. Albert and Company (in 1948; he became the boss in 1955), and the company—under his guidance—grew to become the largest outfit in the home heating business.

He also developed alarm systems and set up a home security company. For a time, with his daughter and son-in-law, he was involved in the early days of Internet development.

Before stepping down in "retirement," Norm ran a fleet of 22 oil trucks, delivering 80,000,000 barrels of heating oil a year.

One of Norm Spector's most important achievements, in human terms, was his employment of hockey great Maurice "Rocket" Richard as his Public Relations vice-president.

Richard, one of the greatest hockey players in history, found himself with a small pension when his playing career was over. The owners of the Canadiens, the Molson Brewery, made no special provision for their team's all-time star. It was Norm who hired him and his company benefited from the player's prominence. S. Albert, in earlier times, had an 80 per cent Jewish clientele. With the Rocket speaking on the company's behalf, business boomed.

Norm is also a man who doesn't forget. As a youth, when he delivered bags of coal, he found himself, covered with coal dust and hungry, turned away from restaurants. However, one kind-hearted waitress, noting his distress, told him to come to the back door of the restaurant, where she served him meals.

In later years, the woman was a waitress at Montreal's legendary Brown Derby Restaurant, and Norm always sat at her tables—leaving handsome tips and periodically rewarding her with a large gift. And the restaurant was where he held numerous meetings. "Breakfast" often lasted more than two hours during which he transacted major business deals.

Today, Norm Spector leads a less hectic life in many ways. But he still turns up every day at his office to handle his affairs. He sold out his share of the oil business some years ago and is now in property development.

His walls are decorated with many highlights of a busy life but he takes more time to, as it were, smell the roses.

The Synagogue Council of Greater Montreal

The Synagogue Council of Greater Montreal (SCGM), now in its 46th year, brings together all of the city's synagogues, represented by their top leadership, under one umbrella. Fred Pellatt is the seventh President of the Council, made up of the Presidents and immediate past presidents of Montreal-area synagogues plus those in Ste. Agathe and Quebec City. All branches of Judaism are represented, other than the chassidic congregations. The Past Presidents of the Council since its inception, in 1959, include:

Harry Berger (founding president)
Moe Seidman
Edward B. Wolkove
Manny Dalfen
Les Satov
Salim Moghrabi (first Sephardic President)
Fred Pellatt (current President)

The 34 congregations represented on the Council are:
Adath Israel - Poale Zedek Anshei Ozeroff Congregation
Beth Hazichoron Synagogue
Beth Israel Beth Aaron Congregation
Beth Tikvah Congregation
Beth Zion Congregation
Chevra Mishnais Jacob Josef Congregation
Chevra Shaas Adath Yeshurun Hadrath Kodesh Shevet Achim Chaverim kol Yisrael D'Bet Abraham Congregation
Communauté Sépharade de la Banlieue ouest de Montréal
Communauté Sépharade Hekhal Shalom
Communauté Sépharade Petah Tikvah
Congregation Beth El
Congregation Beth Hillel
Congregation Beth Ora
Congregation Chevra Kadisha-B'nai Jacob
Congregation Dorshet Emet
Congregation Or Sépharade de Laval
Congregation Sépharade Beth Rambam
Congregation Sépharade Or Hahayim
Congregation Shaar Hashomayim
Congregation Shaar Shalom
Congregation Shomrim Laboker - Beth Yehuda Shaare Tefillah-Beth Hamedrash Hagadol Tifereth Jerusalem

Congregation Zichron Kedoshim
House of Israel
Netivot Haim Congregation
Shaare Zedek Congregation
Shaare Zion Congregation
South Shore Jewish Community
Spanish and Portuguese Congregation
Synagogue Or Sholom
Temple Emanu-El-Beth Sholom
Tifereth Beth David Jerusalem Beth Yitzchok Kenal Yeshurin
Young Israel of Chomedey
Young Israel Montreal
Young Israel of Val Royal

The Members of the Synagogue Council of Greater Montreal, 2005. Presidents in the picture include Les Satov (top row right); Manny Dalfen (top row, second from right), Fred Pellatt (middle of 2nd row); Edward Wolkove, (front row, 2nd from left), Salim Moghrabi (centre, front row).

Every six weeks, the President gathers together Council members to discuss matters of common concern.

While the group is careful to steer clear of any interference in the affairs of individual congregations, they spell out nine areas where a united effort would be productive.

Goals include "uniting all the religious forces of our congregations," strengthening Jewish education, strengthening the congregations themselves through making members of the Jewish community "increasingly aware of the duty and privilege of synagogue affiliation."

The Council goes beyond Montreal Jewry, seeking to work with "established agencies" for the benefit of Jews in distress anywhere, and there is, inevitably, a strong emphasis on assisting the people of Israel.

The wide scope of Council's thinking includes efforts to combat "bigotry and prejudice".

However, probably the most important theme of the Council's programming is aimed at strengthening the synagogue movement. Founding President Harry Berger, speaking in 1962, sounded a warning note when he declared "the centrality of the synagogue position in Jewish life today is being challenged in many quarters." Mr. Berger reminded the Council's annual meeting of the "exalted place the synagogue occupies in Jewish history." Underscoring the organization's agenda, its founding President declared "the synagogue can be effective only to the degree that its council truly represents and speaks for the synagogues of Montreal."

Rabbi Robert Sternberg, speaking to the Council in 1983, underscored the unified support for the group, noting "the only group of synagogue-affiliated Jews in Montreal not represented on the Council are those who are members of chassidic congregations."

Council's first Sephardic president, Salim Moghrabi, described the body's "most important role" as being the place where the synagogues' top leaders can meet and discuss matters of mutual concern.

Gerald Bronfman's Purple Bag

Gerald Bronfman, son of Harry Bronfman (one of Sam's older brothers) originated the idea of the purple bag for Seagram's top-of-the-line whiskey. The bag quickly and positively identified the Seagram's brand. Colourful, with gold trimming, it generally found some other use around the house or office. In New York, when Gerald trotted out his packaging idea, one Seagram's executive, excited and impressed, introduced Gerald as the next Chairman of Seagram's.

Sam Bronfman was furious at the idea that someone, other than one of his sons, Edgar or Charles, would succeed him. Accordingly, a bewildered Gerald's clever idea brought him a letter—and a separation bonus. He was fired! But Gerald didn't sit on his hands. He went into the milk business—and made a fortune.

For decades after he died, Gerald maintained his father's office intact, with a stunning Dutch painting on the wall. To a visitor, it seemed that Harry had just gone down the hall to see someone and would soon reappear. Similarly, Sam Bronfman's office remained untouched for years, including the gold desk set on his desk reading, to acknowledge the plateau reached by Seagram's, "Thanks a billion, Dad," and they had signed it, in gold, Edgar and Charles.

(Gerald Bronfman, no matter what the weather, always wore rubbers on his shoes for fear of catching cold.)

THE TOUYZ FAMILY

The Touyz family traces its origins back to a family of six orthodox Jewish brothers (Tsemach, Kalman, Chaim, Shlomo, Avraham and Iedel) from Lithuania. Around 1880, four emigrated to South Africa where they assumed the name Touyz, and two emigrated to the USA, where Touyz's flourished in Bridgeport, CT. In the USA, they changed the name to Tose, and established a transport business called Tose-Trucking. Leonard Tose was a financier and entrepreneur who lived in Philadelphia, owned the Philadelphia Eagles Football team (1988-1990) and manufactured LHT Maxi-Cube Trucks.

The Touyz Family in Canada

Louis Z. G. Touyz, BDS, MSc (Dent) (Perio and OralMed), FADI, FICD, FPFA, FACD.
Rhian Merry Touyz. BScHons, MB-Bch, PhD
Alexis Robynne Touyz, BA, Dip Homeop
Joshua Gideon Elliot Touyz
Sarah Judith Jean Touyz

Professors Louis Zalman Glick Touyz and Rhian Merry Touyz, and their children Joshua, Sarah and Alexis Touyz, arrived in Montreal Sept. 20, 1991, from Johannesburg, Republic of South Africa, as landed immigrants.

Prof. Louis Z.G. Touyz, born in Riga, Latvia, is the youngest son of Eli Touyz (1899-1969) and Jenny Gene Touyz (nee Glick 1906-1977). He has one sister, Yvonne (Yocheved) and three brothers Valve, Benjamin and Cyril Touyz. Louis was born and educated in Johannesburg. He was recruited, in 1991, as Director and Professor of Periodontics at McGill University Faculty of Dentistry. He trained in South Africa as a Speech Teacher at Trinity College, London, and as a dentist, scientist and a Specialist in Periodontics and Oral Medicine at the University of the Witwatersrand, where he was Senior Specialist and lecturer 1978-1990. He is a practising consulting Specialist in Periodontics, and often acts as a Professional Referee and Arbitrator in disputes. He was awarded Fellowships in The Academy of Dentistry International 1995, The International College of Dentistry 1996, The Pierre Fouchard Academy 1997, and The American College of Dentists 1998. He has published many scientific articles in local and international journals, presented and lectured at International World Professional Congresses. Over 2,000 dentists qualified under his tutelage. From 2001 onward, he has been President of the Men's Association at the Shaar Hashomayim Synagogue. He is also an artist of renown, having exhibited his ceramic work and paintings of Judaica in South Africa and Canada. His work is in the Jewish Museum of South Africa in Johannesburg and has been acquired by major collectors in Australia, USA,

Israel, South Africa and Canada. In 1997, he was presented with The Meritorious Gold Medal of Honour for his artwork from Renaissance Française Société de France.

Prof. Louis Z.G. Touyz

Prof. Rhian M. Touyz (nee Glassman) stems from the family Glazman from Vilna, Lithuania. Her paternal grandfather Glassman and grandmother emigrated to South Africa in the early 20th Century. Her maternal grandfather (Libner) and grandmother emigrated from London UK to Zambia. Rhian is the oldest daughter of Arnold Glassman (Dip. Arch.) and Geraldine (nee Libner) Glassman. Along with sister Amanda and younger brother Stephen Glassman, Rhian was born and educated in Johannesburg, South Africa. She attained her Medical Doctorate training in Medicine at the University of the Witwatersrand 1998 and graduated cum laude with her Ph.D. in 1993. She has received many accolades for her research, including the prestigious Dahl Award for meritorious Research from the American Heart Foundation, 2004. She was a Senior Research Scientist at the Clinical Research Institute of Montreal 1991-2004. She has focused her research on hypertension, and has published many distinguished articles locally and abroad in her field. She is world renowned as a ground-breaking, eminent researcher and is acknowledged as one of the world's leaders in the field of hypertension. She has travelled extensively across the globe as an invited speaker. In 2005, she was awarded a Canada Research Chair Level One and accepted the position as Chief Scientist and Research Director of the Renal Research Laboratory at the Ottawa Health Service Centre at the University of Ottawa, where she also practises as a medical doctor. She was trained in the arts, is a talented artist in her own right, and is an accomplished ballet dancer.

Prof. Rhian M. Touyz

Ben Weider, C.M., C.Q., SBStJ, Ph.D.

Since 1945, Ben Weider and his brother Joe have operated Weider Sports Equipment Limited and Weider Health and Fitness in Canada and the United States. These two companies manufacture and sell their products throughout the world.

The Weider organization has fostered the development of a strong and still-growing fitness and strength-conditioning industry which has provided employment for thousands, as well as a refreshing new approach to health and physical well-being.

In addition, Ben and Joe Weider were instrumental in developing the vitamin, mineral, protein and sports nutrition industry.

Ben Weider is the founder and President of the International Federation of Bodybuilders (IFBB) which he started in Montreal in 1946. The IFBB currently has 171 national affiliates, making it one of the world's largest sporting organizations. Bodybuilding and fitness are considered an important factor in the collective health of citizens.

On January 30, 1998, the International Olympic Committee (IOC) granted official provisional recognition to the IFBB. This recognition is probably the most important of Ben Weider's accomplishments after 52 years of determination and persistence.

The IFBB is a member of the General Association of International Sports Federations (GAISF), the Association of the IOC Recognized International Sports Federations (ARISF), the International Council of Sport Science and Physical Education, and the International Pierre de Coubertin Committee.

The IFBB is recognized by the Olympic Council of Asia and the Supreme Council for Sport in Africa. The IFBB is also recognized and participates in the following Games: the Pan American Games, the Southeast Asia Games, the Caribbean Games, the Arab Games, the South Pacific Games, the African Games and the World Games.

Montrealers Ben (right) and Joe Weider—international figures in the fields of bodybuilding and fitness, with California Governor Arnold Schwarzenegger. The brothers brought Schwarzenegger from Austria to the United States where he went from film stardom to the Governor's mansion.

Honorary Degrees

1997 - Doctor of Humane Letters, Florida State University
1994 - Doctor of Laws, Concordia University, Montreal
1987 - Ph.D. Sports Sciences, United States Sports Academy
1972 - Doctor of Physical Education, Baghdad

Awards and Special Recognition

2004 - The Imperial Order of the Dragon of Annam (knighthood)—His Imperial Highness, Prince Nguyen Phuc Buu Chanh of Vietnam enthusiastically selected Ben Weider to receive the knighthood in recognition of the many years he has been actively involved in charity work, his efforts in educating people worldwide on the positive benefits of physical fitness and the promotion of peace and unity through sports.

The ceremony and presentation took place on July 29, 2004 at the DACOR Bacon House, Washington, DC.

On the 21st of February, Ben Weider was made an Honorary member of the U.S. Marine Corps Station, Miramar Bodybuilding Team, "Dog Team Development."

2003 - Chevalier of the Sovereign Military and Hospitaller Order of Saint John of Jerusalem, Knights of Malta Ecumenical. In January 2003, Ben Weider received this honour from Baron Vladimirovith Kondratovitch, Grand Prior of the Order.

2002 - On June 12, Ben Weider was elected to be a member of the Administration Council of the Ambulance Saint-Jean.

2001 - Ordre de St-Jean. On June 2, Ben Weider was made a member of the Ordre de St-Jean, Canadian Branch.

2000 - Awarded the Legion of Honour (France's most prestigious award, created by the Emperior Napoleon in 1802) by French government decree dated May 15.
Knight of the National Order of Quebec—presented by Provincial Premier Lucien Bouchard.

1999 - Honorary Lieutenant-Colonel 62nd Field Artillery Regiment, Shawinigan Falls, Quebec.
Gold Medal, Palestine (presented by Chairman Yasser Arafat)
Most Influential Sports Figures, placed 48th of 125 (Sport Intern survey)
Honorary President, History on the Net
Officer, 78th Fraser Highlanders of the Frt. St. Helen Garrison.
Honorable Academician, International Academy of Sciences, Education, Industry and Arts, Mountainview, California.

1998 - Honorary Chief Inspector, Montreal Police Department.
Eppes Society Honoree, Florida State University, Tallahassee.

1997 - International Patron, Norfolk Island Museum (South Pacific)
Honorary Colonel, Garde Imperiale of England.
Honorary Member, International Academy of Sciences, Education, Industry and Arts.

1996 - Chairman, Programs Committee, USSA
Honorary President, Arab Physical Culture Federation (Lebanon)
Inductee Quebec Sports Hall of Fame.
Honorary Commander, Montreal SWAT Team.
Honorary Degree, National Academy of Sports and Physical Education, Romania.
Founding Member, Council on Fitness and Sports Health Science, International Chiropractors Association.
Member, Institute on Napoleon and the French Revolution, Florida State University.

1995 - Honorary Ambassador at Large, Guam.
Distinguished Medal of Achievement, Florida State University.
Distinguished Service Award, Napoleonic Institute, Florida State University.
Lifetime Achievement Award of the Governor's Council on Physical Fitness and Sport (presented by Arnold Schwarzenegger).
Pioneer Award, American Academy of Anti-Aging, USA.

1994 - Honorary physical education instructor, Los Angeles Police Department,
Member of the Anti-Aging Medicine Academy.
Torah Award, Montreal

1993 - Honorary President Montreal Convalescent Hospital.
Honorary President YM/YWHAs of Quebec

1992 - Baden Powell Companion, International Scout Foundation
Danny Thomas Founder Award, St. Jude Children's Research Hospital (New England Branch)
Joe and Ben Weider Day, declared by Los Angeles Mayor Bradley.

1991 - Polish Government Order of Merit (signed by Lech Walesa)
Honor Medal, Comenius University, Bratislava, Slovak Republic
Certificate of Merit, Syrian Olympic Committee.
Distinguished Knight's Cross, Graz, Austria.
Fellow of the Royal Society for the Encouragement of Arts, Manufacture and Commerce.
Highest Sports Award, Ministry of Sport for Russia.
Highest Sports Medal, Republic of Lithuania.

1990 - Honorary Marshal, Y.S. Marshal Service, Washington, D.C.

1988 - Silver Medal of Paris.
Honorary Professorship, Shanghai Institute of Physical Education, People's Republic of China.

Cultural Medal from the Minister of Sports, Taipei, Taiwan.
Guest Professor of Peking University, a rare distinction bestowed on Mr. Weider by Zhang Xueshu,
Vice-President, University of Peking, People's Republic of China.

1987 - Maltese Cross; Order of St. John, Knights of Malta.

1986 - Inductee, Maccabea Hall of Fame, Los Angeles, California.

1985 - Lifetime Member, Canadian Bodybuilding Federation.
Member, International Advisory Board, International Police and Fire Athletic Association, Chevy Chase, Maryland.

1984 - Nobel Peace Prize nominee.
Distinguished Service Award, United States Sports Academy.
Queen's Silver Jubilee Medal

1981 - Member, International Council of Sport and Physical Education, Research Committee, USA.

1975 - Order of Canada.

Publications

Qui a tué Napoléon? (Robert Laffont)
The Murder of Napoleon (Congdon Lattes) translated into Chinese, Spanish, Korean, Czech, German, Arabic, Greek, Hebrew, French, Hindi, Dutch, Hungarian, Italian, Japanese, Lithuanian, Norwegian, Polish, Romanian, Russian (six editions—more than 500,000 copies), Slovakian, Swedish, Turkish, Urdu (Pakistan)
Assassination at St. Helena (Mitchell Press)
Assassination at St. Helena Revisited (John Wiley and Sons)
Napoléon, est-il mort empoisonné (Les Éditions Pygmalion)
Napoleon, the Man who Shaped Europe (Spellmount Publishers, London)
La Sagesse de Napoléon (Les Éditions Québecor)
Napoléon, Liberté, Égalité, Fraternité (Les éditions Trois-Pistoles)
Louis Cyr, l'homme le plus fort du monde (six editions, Les éditions Québecor)
Les hommes forts du Québec (Les éditions Trois-Pistoles)
Mangez bien et restez svelte
Jeune toute sa vie

Special Activities

Ben Weider is currently President of the International Napoleonic Society, which has branches in 39 countries. His knowledge about the Emperor Napoleon is legendary, and he is a widely sought lecturer on the subject to history students, including those at Moscow University in 1991, and McGill University in 1994. In June, 1995, Mr. Weider was invited to give a lecture to the officers of SHAPE/NATO at Mons,

Belgium. He has also lectured at Sandhurst Military Academy in London, England, and at the Borodino Military Museum in Borodino, Russia.

In 1975, he journeyed to St. Helena to visit the facility where Napoleon lived the final years of his life.

In 1995, two books by Ben Weider were included in a two-volume set of Napoleonic history, published by the Russian Historical Society. These books, *The Murder of Napoleon* and *La Sagesse de Napoléon*, were included along with highlights from Leo Tolstoy's *War and Peace* and a book about Napoleon by Alexandre Dumas. Over 500,000 copies were sold.

In September 1995, the Florida State University created the Ben Weider Eminent Scholar Chair in Napoleonic History. The University now has the ability to promote Napoleonic history and to encourage travel by students in the context of their Napoleonic research.

In September, 1999, Ben Weider lectured to more than 200 officers at the Royal Canadian Mounted Police headquarters in Montreal, during which he explained how he determined that Napoleon was poisoned rather than accepting the official claim he died of cancer.

In October, 1997, Ben Weider gave a lecture and a press conference in Paris, organized at the Cultural Centre of the Canadian Embassy on the topic of the poisoning of Napoleon. The French Minister of Culture, Alain Valery Coquerel, was present as well as His Excellency Prince Murat, who gave the opening address.

In September, 1987, Mr. Weider was a guest of the Russian Parliament at the marking of the 350th anniversary of the founding of Moscow.

In September 1997, Mr. Weider was invited by the Director of the State Borodino War and History Museum and Reserve to attend the 185th anniversary of the 1812 Battle of Borodino. Prior to the re-enactment, Mr. Weider addressed 100,000 Russian spectators who had come to see a re-play of the battle between the French, led by Napoleon, and the Russians, led by General Kutusoc. Mr. Weider also spoke to Russian historians about the poisoning of Napoleon.

In February, 1987, Ben Weider was the keynote speaker at the 27th Consortium on Revolutionary Europe, organized by the Louisiana State University in Baton Rouge, Louisiana.

In March 1996, Mr. Weider was the keynote speaker on "The Assassination of Napoleon at St. Helena During His Exile" at the 26th Consortium on Revolutionary Europe, held under the auspices of the Georgia Southern University in Savannah, Georgia.

In his more than 40 years in the field of fitness and sports, Ben Weider has become an international authority figure whose philosophy, books, courses, nutritional findings and reports on athletic performance and general fitness have been recognized throughout the world.

Through his Foundation, Mr. Weider has made major contributions to international sport and has been a generous contributor and supporter of fitness programs in many countries. He has donated complete training gyms with state-of-the-art equipment to encourage young people and assist institutions involved in sports research and training. Gyms have been donated in the following countries—the USA, Canada, Germany (The University of Cologne), Lebanon, Syria, Israel (the Israeli Olympic Committee), the People's Republic of China, Egypt, Jordan and Palestine.

A complete state-of-the-art Weider gym was donated in August, 1994, to the Los Angeles Police Department. Ben and Joe Weider also donated bodybuilding gyms to each of the 18 police stations throughout Los Angeles. The Los Angeles Police Department made Ben and Joe Honorary Physical Education Instructors of the Police Department.

Fully-equipped Weider Gyms were also donated to the following non-profit organizations: The Canadian Institute for Neuro-Integrative Development (Montreal), Stanstead College (Stanstead, Quebec), Lower Canada College (Montreal), McGill University (Montreal), Allan Memorial Juvenile Division of the Royal Victoria Hospital (Montreal), Portage Foundation Drug Rehabilitation Centre (Montreal), Lower Canada College Selwyn House (Montreal), Centre Immaculée-Conception (Montreal), Youth For Christ (Winnipeg), and CEGEP Edouard Montpetit (Longueuil, Quebec).

In 1998, Ben Weider donated full, state-of-the-art physical fitness and bodybuilding gyms to the City Hall in Tel Aviv, Israel; The Israeli Army Fitness Centre; The Shanghai Institute of Physical Education and Sport; the Lebanese Olympic Committee, and the Quebec Police Training School in Nicolet, Quebec. (Mr. Weider was chairman of the ceremony).

Ben Weider has been a consistent supporter of the Montreal YMHA, supplying them with equipment for bodybuilding gyms and supporting them financially. In response to this support, the Montreal Jewish Community Centre changed its name to the Ben Weider Jewish Community Centre.

Furthermore, the Bais Chaya Mushka Seminary named their new facility the Ben Weider Educational Centre.

In 1999, he helped raise funds and made a large personal donation to Montreal's Cardinal Turcotte to help in the renovation of the main Cathedral.

Ben Weider is most certainly a Citizen of the World.

EDWARD B. WOLKOVE, C.A.

Edward B. Wolkove is a Montreal accountant who, in addition to a distinguished professional career, has played a diversified role in the Jewish community and beyond.

The positions he has held encapsulize his story:

President of the Synagogue Council of Greater Montreal
Both President and Treasurer of Canadian Jewish Congress—Quebec
Vice-President, Member of the Executive and Treasurer of Canadian Jewish Congress —National.
Vice-President/Treasurer, Beth Hamedrash Hagadol Congregation
Chair of the Cote St. Luc Division, Combined Jewish Appeal
Treasurer of the Association for Canadian Jewish Studies—National
Treasurer, Jewish Community Council of Montreal
Treasurer, Liberal Party of Canada, Mount Royal Riding
Treasurer, World Conference of Religion for Peace Canada
Treasurer and Member of the Executive, Beth Zion Congregation
Member of the Boards of Federation CJA, Canadian Council of Christians and Jews—Quebec, Jewish Education Council, Montreal Israel Bond Committee
Treasurer, Hebrew Culture Organization of Canada

While those are past positions, he remains extremely active currently as:

Co-President, Muslim-Jewish Dialogue of Montreal
Chair, Masada Checkpoint, March to Jerusalem
Treasurer and member of the Executive, Christian Jewish Dialogue of Montreal
Treasurer and Member of the Executive, Synagogue Council of Greater Montreal
Treasurer of both the Eastern Region of the Canadian Zionist Federation and Canadian Friends of Raoul Wallenberg
Member of the Executive, and Chair of the Religious and Interreligious Committee of Canadian Jewish Congress—Quebec
Member of the Board of the World Conference on Religion for Peace—Canada

In addition, he is active in the Combined Jewish Appeal as a member of the Leadership Team and the Executive Elan Division, and sits on the Professional Advisory Committee of the Jewish Community Foundation.

Edward B. Wolkove, C. A.

Ed Wolkove delights in recalling happy times—serving as Chair of the Reunion Committee of Baron Byng High, Class of '39, and Co-Chair of the Reunion Committee, McGill University School of Commerce, Class of '48.

In between these educational packages, he served in the Canadian Army 1942-1945.

In 1993, the Government of Canada honoured Mr. Wolkove with the Commemorative Medal marking the 125th Anniversary of Confederation, and Canadian Jewish Congress—Quebec presented him with its Ezekiel Hart Award, in 2003, for "promoting interfaith relations."

In addition to all that, Edward Wolkove is a partner in the Chartered Accounting Firm of Perreault Wolman Grzywacz & Co., and a Life Member of the Order of Chartered Accountants of both Quebec and Ontario.

Hirsch Wolofsky

Twenty-four-year-old Hirsch Wolofsky disembarked from a vessel in Montreal Harbour, in 1900—an immigrant from Poland who was destined to become one of the leading architects of the Montreal Jewish Community.

Seven years after his arrival, Wolofsky had worked his way up from peddling, on a bicycle, to become proprietor of a fruit store on the southeast corner of St. Lawrence Boulevard and Guilbault. However, his 7-year-old son, Philip, playing with matches, set the building on fire. With the insurance from the fire, Hirsch Wolofsky audaciously set out to make a dream a reality. He wanted to establish a Yiddish-language newspaper in Montreal.

Publisher and community leader Hirsch Wolofsky

"Within a month," Wolofsky wrote in his autobiography, "*The Eagle* was a functioning journal, located at 508 St. Lawrence Boulevard, and boasting the first Jewish linotype machine in Canada."

After five years of struggling to keep it afloat, acceptance became so strong that he began publishing the English-language *Jewish Chronicle*.

With these two publications, particularly the one reaching the rapidly increasing Yiddish-speaking immigrant population, Wolofsky was able to spur the Jewish community into creating new agencies to serve the growing and changing needs of its constituents.

The Eagle was at the service of the community and many synagogues, landsmanshaften, philanthropic, educational and cultural groups owed their very existence to the opportunities provided by *The Eagle* for them to reach the public. He was a strong supporter of Jewish education and was president of United Talmud Torahs when they constructed their first building.

The outstanding Canadian Jewish leader, H. M. Caiserman, wrote of his friend, and his newspaper:

"From its first day, *The Jewish Daily Eagle* has been the spokesman of the Community, the school for its writers and the builder of Canadian Jewry. Every communal activity needed the press to reach the community."

Hirsch Wolofsky was a leading figure in building Montreal's strong network of service organizations.

He helped push for a Jewish Public Library and found its first home on Esplanade. He was one of the key people in the formation of the Federation of Jewish Philanthropies (now known as Federation CJA).

He proposed the idea of a Jewish Immigration Society. He served on the committee, in 1929, responsible for proposing the creation of a Jewish hospital.

He urged the national community to form what became Canadian Jewish Congress, and he was a vigorous Zionist, who visited Palestine several times and wrote about the burgeoning Jewish community there.

When Hirsch's son, Max, was honoured at the 60th anniversary of JIAS, the legendary Doctor Joseph Kage paid tribute to Max and, at the same time, to the whole family:

"The late Hirsch Wolofsky was the most astute, intelligent and committed community leader. Max, the son, represents the "hemshekh." This continuity of communal history emphasizes the idea that the controlling factors of historic events lie not always only in the impersonal circumstances of external environment but also in the heart's response."

The Wolofsky Family

Sarah Bercovitch Wolofsky and Hirsch had a large family—seven children—Philip (or Felix), Daniel, Max, Moses, Saul, Sophie and Miriam—five sons and two daughters.

Hirsch Wolofsky's commitment to the continuity of the Montreal Jewish community, and to social justice, was passed on to his family. Several of his children and grandchildren have made their contributions in Montreal. Philip joined the Jewish Legion in World War I and then returned to work with his father at *The Eagle* where he was very active in helping immigrants settle here. His daughter, Sophie Crestohl, was a leader of Hadassah and founded Canadian ORT. Daniel ran the business end of *The Eagle*.

Max Wolofsky followed in his father's footsteps.

Max had begun his career as a lawyer in New York where he was one of the founders of the International Association of Immigration and Nationality Lawyers. He served as President of Gad Lodge, Free Sons of Israel and of Jordan Lodge, B'nai Brith. After the untimely death of his brother Philip, he returned to Montreal to eventually completely take over as publisher of *The Eagle* and the *Chronicle*. He became deeply immersed in communal life, serving on many boards, and assuming the presidency of JIAS, the Rabbinical College of Lubavitch, and the General Chairmanship of the Israel Bond Organization.

Moses (Bill Walsh) moved to Ontario where he devoted his life to improving the lives of Workers and First Nations. Shalom (Sam Walsh) was convinced that the welfare of humanity could better be served under a socialist system, and lived his life accordingly.

Miriam Cooperberg was the darling of the family whose love for all kept the family together.

While many of the Wolofsky grandchildren have left Montreal, several have served this community well.

Philip's daughter Goldie Eshkazi served as president of the Sisterhood of Temple Emanu-El; his son Jack became President of Dorshei Emet, the Reconstructionist Synagogue.

Sophie Crestohl's son Harvey rose in the ranks of B'nai Brith Canada from president of two lodges, to chairman of the city council, to national president of the organization.

Max's daughter Merle (Frankel) was founder president of Centennial Chapter B'nai Brith Canada and the first female president of the Hillel Foundation of Montreal. She was then appointed Executive Director of Jewish People's and Peretz Schools and Bialik High School.

Women's Federation/Combined Jewish Appeal

From the Montreal Jewish community's earliest days, women took a leadership role in planning and providing humanitarian services. At a period in history when women were expected to take care of the home and the children, and obey their husbands, Jewish women were breaking the mould. Often, men were the nominal heads of organizations but it was women who met most of the human needs.

In 1877, the Ladies Hebrew Benevolent Society was formed. It received an annual grant from the province, a yearly grant from the City and District Bank, and raised additional funds through concerts and bazaars.

The concept of a hospital to serve the Jewish community came from Mrs. Taube Kaplan. That led first to the formation of the Hebrew Maternity Hospital in 1916 and, 18 years later, to the creation of the Jewish General Hospital. When Lucy (Mrs. Allan) Bronfman suggested that a ward be named in honour of Mrs. Kaplan, Taube was horrified that her work would be so publicly acknowledged and suggested, instead, to name the ward in honour of a great Jewish figure in history.

In 1917, with the formation of the Federation, women continued to take an important but underplayed role. However, in 1923, when Federation ran into a financial crisis, a woman led the "Save the Federation" Campaign. Mrs. Jacob Elkin formed a Women's Committee and campaigned on the slogan "Wear last year's hat (to synagogue on the High Holidays) and give the cost of a new one to Federation."

Thanks largely to Mrs. Elkin's vigorous leadership, the Campaign was a success and Federation has never looked back. (And, by the way, everyone wore a new hat on Rosh Hashanah.)

In 1931, a Women's Division of Federation was established as a permanent committee and the community's First Lady at that time, Saidye (Mrs. Samuel) Bronfman, was its first chair.

Chairs, Women's Campaign CJA

1931-1933	Mrs. Saidye Bronfman, O.B.E.
1934-1936	Dorothy Block
1937-1939	Rosa Singer
1940-1943	Rhoda Leopold
1944-1947	Ethel Klein
1948	Celia Isaacs
1949-1950	Lillian Jacobs
1951-1952	Mildred Lande, C.M.
1953-1954	Pauline Coshof
1955-1956	Ghita Roll
1957-1958	Bobby Barkoff
1959-1960	Rhoda Cohen
1961-1962	Lee Gertsman

Reorganization

In 1963, Women's Division was reorganized as Women's Federation of Combined Jewish Appeal, with "responsibilities for education and interpretation" as well as campaign. Mrs. Dorothy (J. Julius) Block was named its first President.

Presidents, Women's Federation CJA	Chairs, Women's Campaign CJA
1964-1966 - Dorothy Block	1963 - Ruth Nadler
	1964 - Bess Pascal
	1965 - Hon. Sheila Finestone, P.C.
1966-1967 - Mildred Lande, C.M.	1966 - Irene Lande
	1967 - Faiga Fisher
1968-1969 - Lee Gertsman	1968 - Rosetta Elkin
	1969 - Phyllis Waxman, O.Q.
1969-1971 - Hon. Sheila Finestone, P.C.	1970 - Dodo Heppner
	1971 - Neri Bloomfield
1971-1973 - Dodo Heppner	1972 - Maxine Sigman
	1973 - Nettie Weinstein
1973-1975 — Phyllis Waxman, O.Q	1974 - Kappy Flanders
	1975 - Irma Polisuk
1976-1978 - Faiga Fisher	1976 - Leila Paperman
	1977 - Anne Nadler

Mildred (Mrs. Bernard) Lande became the first woman General Chairman of the Combined Jewish Appeal in 1978.

1978-1980 - Shirley Rabinovitch	1978 - Marilyn Blumer
	1979 - Zelda Thow
1980-1982 - Dorothy Greenbaum	1980 - Esther Landsman
	1981 - Shirley Goldfarb
1982-1984 - Rhoda Granatstein	1982 - Lois Leiff
	1983 - Shirley Rabinovitch

Doris Weiser Small

Elaine Mintz

Rosalyn Wolfe

Dodo Heppner became the first woman President of Federation 1983-1985.

1984-1986 - Ruth Ballon
1986-1988 - Elaine R. Goldstein
1988-1990 - Annette Oliel Ama
1990-1992 - Laya Feldman
1992 - 1994 - Diane Sasson
1994-1996 - Monette Malewski
1996-1998 - Bunny Lechter
1998-2000 - Rhoda Vineberg
2000-2003 - Jewel Lowenstein
2003-2005 - Sue Carol Isaacson
2005-2007 - Marlene King

1984 - Bernice Brownstein
1985 - Dorothy Greenbaum
1986 - Rosalind Goodman
1987 - Joan Lazarus
1988 - Carole Ann Levine
1989 - Doris Weiser Small
1990 - Roslyn Wolfe
1991 - Joyce Tanner
1992 - Rhoda Vineberg
1993 - Lily Ivanier
1994 - Dale Boidman
1995 - Evelyn Bloomfield Schachter
1996 - Etty Bienstock
1997 - Alta Levenson
1998 - Jewel Lowenstein
1999 - Harriet Muroff
2000 - Alice Raby
2001 - Sue Carol Isaacson
2002 - Marlene King
2003 - Elaine Mintz
2004 - Helen Levy
2005 - Elaine Dubrovsky
2006 - Sarah Rubin

In 1983, the Sephardic Women developed their own campaign, with their own chair.

Chairs, Sephardic Women—Combined Jewish Appeal:

1983 - Fabienne Marelli
1984 - Aline Malka
1985 - Annette Amar
1986 - Coty Benchetrit Kalfon
1987 - Simone Banon
1988 - Fiby Benchaya
1989 Anne Medalsy
1990 - Maryse Ohayon
1991 - Sylvia Toledano
1992 - Joelle Khalfa
1993 - Raymonde Abenaim
1994 - Linda Amram
1995 - Gigi Amar
1996 - Margot Spiegelman
1997 - Therese Attias
1998 - Rita Guindi
1999 - Pascale Hasen
2000 - Rachel Alloul
2001 - Arlene Abitan
2002 - Patricia Lallouz Malka
2003 - Betty Elkaim Cohen
2004 - Camille Cohen
2005 - Yvette Fanny Ettinger

During its long history, Women's Federation/Combined Jewish Appeal has had only three Directors—Mitzi Lowy, Rosalind Brott and, since 1987, Beverlee Ashmele.

In 1995, Mrs. Ashmele was presented with the Federation CJA Award for Professional Excellence. And in 1999, Keren Hayesod named her winner of its prestigious international S. J. Kreutner Award.

APPENDIX

Montreal Jews who have been awarded the Order of Canada:

Monroe Abbey
David Azrieli
Clara Z. Balinsky
Manuel G. Batshaw
Samuel Berger
Benjamin Beutel
Charles Bronfman C.C.
Edward Bronfman O.C.
Samuel Bronfman C.C.
Alexander Brott
Boris Brott O.C.
Lotte Brott
Gordon Brown
Morton Brownstein
Leonard Cohen C.C.
Maxwell Cohen O.C.
Marvin Corber
Irwin Cotler O.C.
Maxwell Cummings
Mitzi M.S. Dobrin O.C.
Pauline Donalda
Sheila L. Fischman
Samuel O. Freedman O.C.
Morrie Gelfand
Samuel Gesser
Allan. B. Gold O.C.
Phil Gold C.C.
Sheila Goldbloom
Victor Goldbloom C.C.
H. Carl Goldenberg O.C.
David Goltzman O.C.
Harold Greenberg O.C.
Harry Halton O.C..
Saul Hayes O.C.
Michal Hornstein
Isin Ivanier O.C.
Paul Ivanier
Naim Kattan O.C..
Sandra Kolber
Sheila Gordon Kussner O.C.
Phyllis Lambert C.C.
Lawrence Lande
Mildred Lande
Irving Layton O.C.
Boris G. Levine
Frederick Loewy
Edith H.J. Low-Beer
Jacob M. Lowy
Eric Maldoff
Richard Margolese
Victor Melnikoff
Ronald Melzack O.C.
Brenda Milner C.C.
Henry Mintzberg O.C.
Louis Muhlstock O.C.
Sarah Paltiel
Arthur Pascal
Tania Plaw
Isidore Pollack
Mordecai Richler C.C.
Alan Rose
Sara Rosenfeld
George J. Rosengarten O.C.
Moshe Safdie O.C.
Barbara Seal
Alvin Segal
Herbert Siblin
Samuel Solomon O.C.
Ethel Stark
H. Arnold Steinberg
Abraham Stern
Max Stern
Edith Strauss
Herschel Victor
Arthur Vineberg O.C.
Philip Vineberg O.C.
Mark Wainberg O.C.
Dora Wasserman
Ben Weider
William Weintraub O.C.
Jonathon Wener
Joel Wolfe
Leo Yaffe O.C.

The Index